WILLS AND PROBATE

WILLS AND PROBATE

CONSUMERS' ASSOCIATION

Which? Books are commissioned and researched by
Consumers' Association and published by
Which? Ltd, 2 Marylebone Road, London NW1 4DF
email address: guide.reports@which.net

Distributed by The Penguin Group:
Penguin Books Ltd, 27 Wrights Lane, London W8 5TZ

Revised by:
Paul Elmhirst (England and Wales)
Dr David Nichols (Scotland)
Alastair J. Rankin (Northern Ireland)

First edition 1967
New edition March 1997

British Library Cataloguing-in-Publication Data
A catalogue record for this book is available from the British Library

ISBN 0 85202 643 9

For a full list of Which? books, please write to
Which? Books, Castlemead, Gascoyne Way,
Hertford X, SG14 1LH, or access our web site
at http://www.which.net

Typographic design by Paul Saunders
Cover design by Ridgeway Associates
Cover photograph by Peter Chadwick
Typeset by Saxon Graphics Ltd, Derby
Printed in England by Clays Ltd, St Ives plc

CONTENTS

FOREWORD   7

1   WHY YOU SHOULD MAKE A WILL   9
D-i-y or using a solicitor; inheritance tax;
lifetime gifts; saving tax

2   MAKING A WILL   31
Choosing executors, guardians, beneficiaries

3   WHAT TO SAY IN A WILL   43
Examples of wills in different circumstances,
and explanations; signing the will, where to
keep it; alterations and codicils, revocation

4   IN SCOTLAND   71
Legal rights; revocation

5   PROBATE   77

     TABLE OF ESSENTIAL STEPS   84

6   THE ADMINISTRATION OF AN ESTATE   87
First formalities; valuation of assets, of house,
of shares; pensions, income tax refund; debts;
finance for inheritance tax, finalising the
valuation; probate forms, probate fees, at the
probate registry, paying inheritance tax,
payment by instalments; obtaining the grant;
collecting assets and paying creditors; income
tax and Capital Gains Tax; distribution
according to the will, estate accounts

7   DISTRIBUTION ON INTESTACY   180

8   IN SCOTLAND, CONFIRMATION   192
Joint property, confirmation forms, inventory,
taking the oath and paying tax, steps if there is
no will, small estates, debts and legal rights,
transfer of house

9   DISTRIBUTION ON INTESTACY IN SCOTLAND   206

10   WILLS AND PROBATE IN NORTHERN IRELAND   212

APPENDIX I (NORTHERN IRELAND):
LAND REGISTRY ASSENT FORM   221

APPENDIX II (NORTHERN IRELAND):
LAND REGISTRY REGISTRATION FORM   226

ADDRESSES   229

INDEX   231

Throughout this book for 'he' read 'he or she'

*** Indicates that the address and telephone number will be
found in the Addresses section on page 229**

FOREWORD

DEATH is a subject people do not like to think about. Many people defer, until it is too late, deciding what is to happen to their possessions when they die, and making a will.

This book is intended to help at two separate stages. First, it explains how to make a will in a simple case, including a description of what not to do, what to include and how the will must be signed and witnessed. Secondly, the book describes the administration by the executors of the estate of someone who has died leaving a will. Here, too, only a straightforward case is described, but this is done in some detail, to give the full picture. What happens when there is no will is also explained.

While most people who write their own wills or administer the estates of others are able to do so quite successfully, without any deep knowledge of the law, it is as well to be aware that there are some thirty Acts of Parliament which provide a legal framework within which estates and trusts are administered. Some of the rules are very strict but others can be modified. The Trustee Act 1925 and the Administration of Estates Act 1925 are just two of the more important Acts. If you hit a problem, do seek advice.

The Probate Registry provides a special procedure to deal with laymen who wish to act as personal representatives without having a solicitor. This book supplements this by explaining not only the Probate Registry procedure but also what goes before and what comes after.

This book is not concerned with complicated inheritance tax

(IHT) saving or tax avoidance issues, but the basic rules relating to IHT are described because, in most cases, a will cannot be properly considered without also considering the tax implications. Circumstances appropriate for substantial savings of tax are mentioned, particularly where tax can be saved by a fairly simple course of action. To implement some of the more complicated schemes, however, you would need to get the professional advice of a lawyer, accountant or other financial adviser. The tax savings should be greater than the cost involved.

This book explains the law and procedure in England and Wales, and briefly explains the main differences which apply in Scotland and Northern Ireland in separate chapters.

CHAPTER 1

WHY YOU SHOULD MAKE A WILL

FOR most people, what happens to their property and family when they die is a matter of some importance, but some have an unconscious fear of making a will: they do not wish to consider their death, as if to do so were to tempt providence. It is also something which many people have, quite simply, just not got around to.

Irrespective of the amount of property which a person has at death, if he dies without making a will, the law automatically dictates what is to happen to his property, without any opportunity of considering what the wishes of the deceased would have been. It could happen, by chance, that a wealthy person need not make a will in order to have his wishes fulfilled by the rules which would operate automatically, or that someone who has only a few hundred pounds must make a will if he is to avoid all his property being forfeited to the Crown.

Intestacy

When a person dies without having made a will, the law says that he has died 'intestate'. His estate, that is all his property (after deducting all the debts and liabilities which he owed at his death and which are payable out of his estate), is divided among members of his family according to rules laid down in the Administration of Estates Act. This applies to anyone whose domicile at the time of his death is in England or Wales, wherever that person actually died. If, however, the deceased owned land abroad, the situation can be very complicated. A person's domicile is in whatever country he regards as his real and permanent home; this does not necessarily depend on where he is actually living. Also, the fact that he might, for example, be on holiday in a foreign country at the time of his death does not affect this in any way.

The detailed rules governing the distribution of the property of someone who dies intestate are dealt with in Chapters 7 and 9. The following is a brief summary so that you can see how strict the laws are, and why you should make a will.

Married couple

When there is a husband and wife and all the possessions of the one who dies come to less than £125,000, everything goes to the surviving spouse, irrespective of whether there are any children. Where the value of the estate is more than that, the position becomes more complicated.

If there are children, the surviving spouse is entitled to the first £125,000 and the household contents and personal effects of the deceased person (he or she is not necessarily entitled to keep the house if that is worth more than £125,000). The rest of the estate has to be divided into two equal parts, one of which will go to the children to be divided equally between them. If they are not yet eighteen, it will be held on trust for their benefit until they attain the age of eighteen. The other half has to go into what is called a trust, the effect of which is that the surviving spouse will have a life interest and therefore will, until his or her own death, receive only the income from that half of the rest of the estate. The income might take the form of rents from houses, for example, or dividends on investments and so on. But he or she is not entitled to use the capital of that property, which will ultimately also go to the children on the death of their surviving parent.

With an estate of more than £125,000, if there are no children but a parent or brother or sister of the deceased is still alive, the surviving spouse will receive the first £200,000 of the estate, plus the household contents and personal effects, and one-half of the rest. The other half of the rest of the estate will go to the parents of the deceased person or the brothers and sisters if there is no living parent.

The intestacy rules apply equally to a husband and a wife.

Unmarried people

If a person without husband or wife dies leaving children, then all of the property will go equally to the children.

The estate of an unmarried man or woman without children goes his or her parents, and is divided between them if they are both still alive. If they have died before him, his brothers and sisters will share his estate. If there are none, his grandparents will share it and if they are dead, his aunts and uncles will share the estate. The children (legitimate, illegitimate, adopted – the law makes no distinction) of someone in this order of priority who has died take the share in the estate which their parent would have received had he or she survived the deceased. However, the field of potential beneficiaries of an intestate person is limited to grandparents and their descendants: more distant relatives are not entitled to inherit property. If there are no grandparents or any of their descendants surviving, all the property will go to the Crown, unless the person has made a will.

The fact that a couple have lived together for many years gives no automatic entitlement to the estate of the first to die. A divorced person is treated as one with no surviving spouse.

The need to make a will

Even if, under the intestacy rules, the property you own today would go to the people you would wish, it is impossible to guess in which order the deaths of a husband and wife will occur, and how long there will be between them. It is therefore quite possible that, without a will, the property may not go to the people whom you might have assumed would automatically benefit. Also, your financial position could alter substantially between now and the time when you die: you may become wealthier, or worse off, either of which could mean that you should make a will. The value of your property might increase merely because of inflation so that property worth under £125,000 now could be worth considerably more than £125,000 in a few years' time.

A man also has to consider the position which could arise after his death if, under the rules of intestacy, his widow is entitled to only a life interest in part of his estate. This means that she is not entitled to have the use of the capital which might be necessary simply to maintain her standard of living if the income is not enough in the first place or if, through inflation or reduced interest rates, the income becomes too small for her to live on.

In an intestacy, stringent restrictions are placed on the investments which are authorised by law; they may therefore not necessarily be the investments which would quite properly be advised for the best management of the funds. In a will, these restrictions can be removed, so that a man can give his widow a chance of a better income, and vice versa.

A greater problem can also arise if a husband and wife are killed together, in some common accident, leaving young children behind. The children would be able to receive the capital to which they were entitled only when they became eighteen. Until that time, the property would have to be held in trust for them. In the meantime it would have to be invested, and the restrictions on the kind of investments that can be selected might prevent the property being dealt with as flexibly and advantageously for the benefit of the children as might have been wished. Making a will can give greater freedom regarding investments, and the children could be better off.

Some people believe that a cohabitee can benefit under the intestacy rules. This is not the case. If you wish to provide for a cohabitee, you must make a will. The description 'common-law spouse' is not recognised by the rules of intestacy.

A will can also include things such as funeral wishes, appointment of guardians for children and the passing down of specific items, such as family heirlooms and small gifts to express gratitude for friendship or other kindness during your life. It can be used to express a number of other provisions and wishes. Some of these may not be binding on the people concerned, but they are a useful way of recording your views and wishes.

If you make a will, you can also dictate who are going to be your executors, the people responsible for administering your estate and looking after all your affairs after your death. If there is no will, the law dictates, usually, that your nearest relatives will take on the task of managing your estate (in this case, they are called administrators). You may prefer to specify someone to look after all your concerns – a relative or friend, say, or your solicitor – but to do this, it is essential that you make a will.

Do-it-yourself?

There is no legal requirement that a will should be drawn up or witnessed by a solicitor and quite a number of people do in fact make their own will.

If you are thinking of using a printed form bought in a stationer's shop or elsewhere and making your will by filling in the blanks, make sure that the form is not misleading but appropriate for your special circumstances (the gaps and blanks in the form may be too large or too small for your precise intentions, for example, which can lead to problems). It may be better to avoid the forms and to prepare the document yourself in the way we describe.

The one thing worse than not making a will at all is making a mess of making a will. Many lawyers would say that they can make more money out of poor home-made wills than they do out of drawing up wills for clients. There is probably some truth in this. There are many ways in which people who prepare and sign their own will can go wrong. This can, later, lead to long and expensive court cases to resolve the matter, with enormous legal fees for the lawyers, which can reduce by staggering amounts the size of the estate to which the beneficiaries are entitled.

A will is a technical legal document; it is not surprising that some laymen go astray when they try to make a will unaided. This book explains all the steps necessary to make your will properly, how to word particular clauses and provisions and also how to sign and witness the document properly. But if you have any doubts, you should seek a solicitor's advice.

When to use a solicitor

A solicitor is likely to charge anything from £30 to £100 for preparing a will in a normal case, depending on the circumstances such as, for example, the complexity of the provisions and whether complicated tax-planning clauses are involved. Ask beforehand how much you are likely to be charged.

If your disposable income is less than £75 per week, or you receive income support or family credit and your savings are within certain limits, you will be entitled to receive free legal advice under the green form scheme. Unfortunately the green form scheme does not cover the making of wills unless, as well as being eligible under the green form scheme, you also fall into one of the following categories:

- you are over 70 years old
- you are seriously handicapped, deaf, blind or dumb
- you are the parent of a child who fits into the above category
- you are a single parent wanting to appoint a guardian for your child.

You should always seek advice from a solicitor for making a will if:

- you are receiving an income from a family trust under which you have the right to determine, by your own will, who should benefit from that trust property on your death (this is called a power of appointment)
- your permanent home is in a foreign country, or
- you are resident in England or Wales and there is foreign property involved
- you have made any large gifts during your lifetime
- your estate is likely to exceed £215,000.

You should also consult a solicitor if what you own includes any particularly complicated types of property, for example:

- a business which you are carrying on either on your own or in partnership with other people
- a farm
- shares in a private family company
- if you are involved in any Lloyd's underwriting syndicate

- if you share a property with someone who is not your spouse.

It is essential to consult a solicitor if there are any particular complications in your own personal situation, such as being separated but not divorced from your wife or husband, or in any case where you intend greatly to benefit other people to the exclusion of your spouse or children.

You should also seek a solicitor's advice if, rather than making an outright gift to someone, you wish to create a life interest by specifying that a person should be entitled to benefit from your property only during his or her life and you wish to specify to whom the property will go when that person has died.

A solicitor's advice can also be useful where the estate is large, to consider the various inheritance tax complications and any provisions which might be desirable to save tax and therefore pass more benefit from your estate to members of your family. In very small estates, there is unlikely to be any inheritance tax charge unless you also benefit from a trust.

Anything unusual in your financial or family situation should be regarded as a reason for going to see a solicitor before making a will. Only where your affairs are straightforward should you contemplate trying to do it yourself.

Before considering different types of wills and all the formalities required to ensure that the will is duly and legally executed, it is necessary to understand the essential provisions of inheritance tax, the tax payable when a person dies or, in certain cases, when a person makes a gift.

Inheritance tax

Inheritance tax is the only form of tax or duty imposed on the death of a person whose domicile is in the UK. For many years the tax was known as estate duty; in 1975 this was changed to capital transfer tax, which affected not only the property which passed from one person to another on a person's death but was also a tax on most gifts that people made in their own lifetimes.

Following the Finance Act 1986, capital transfer tax was abolished and a new tax, called inheritance tax (IHT), replaced it. This tax relates mainly to property passing between one person and another as a result of a person's death.

Lifetime gifts

Inheritance tax affects transfers of property on death, and certain transfers made within seven years before the date of death. The taxation of lifetime gifts between people is complex, but offers advantageous tax exemptions. This should be an incentive to make use of the provisions for tax-free lifetime gifts, while they exist, as the rules could be changed at any time.

Some gifts which a person may make in his lifetime will, even so, be chargeable to inheritance tax. These include a gift to a company, or gifts to certain trusts called 'discretionary trusts' (which means that trustees will hold the property and will have a discretion as to who can benefit from that property). However, subject to 'the seven-year rule', gifts made by one individual to another, or to a trust where another person is entitled to the income, or to a trust that benefits children until they reach an age not exceeding twenty-five years for their maintenance and education, or for a disabled person, are not taxable. Advice should, however, be taken as to income tax and capital gains tax (CGT) consequences. The beneficiary should also be made aware of the risks if the donor does not survive for seven years.

The seven-year rule

IHT is a tax on the value of a person's estate at the date of his death. To prevent people giving away all their property immediately before they die, and so avoid the tax, the rules provide that tax is payable not only on all the property which a deceased person has when he dies but also on all the gifts which he made in the last seven years before his death. If the deceased person retained an interest in the gifted property, he will lose the benefit of the seven-year rule.

If a gift has been made and the donor then dies within seven years, the beneficiary will have to pay the tax which now becomes due. If significant amounts are involved, it would certainly be wise for the beneficiary to take out a form of term life insurance payable to the beneficiary so that, if the donor dies within the seven-year period, the policy will provide an amount equal to the tax payable.

Inheritance tax on death

On a person's death, inheritance tax is charged on the value of the deceased person's net estate, that is all his property and assets less all his liabilities and debts. The value of a person's estate includes the full capital value of all property in which he had a life interest or from which he had any benefit or was entitled to the income. The amount of any gift made up to seven years prior to the death is also added to give the total value upon which IHT will be levied.

Before 15 March 1988, the rate of IHT varied from 30% to 60% depending on the size of the estate.

Since 15 March 1988 the rate of IHT has remained at 40%, but the nil-rate band has varied as follows:

date	nil-rate band
15 March 1988–5 April 1989	£110,000
6 April 1989–5 April 1990	£118,000
6 April 1990–5 April 1991	£128,000
6 April 1991–9 March 1992	£140,000
10 March 1992–5 April 1995	£150,000
6 April 1995–5 April 1996	£154,000
6 April 1996–5 April 1997	£200,000
6 April 1997 onwards	£215,000

Usually, a new set of tables is published each year, changing the bands at which higher rates become payable. Even if the one-only rate of IHT (40%) does not change, there may still be an increase in the nil-rate band in accordance with inflation. It is essential to realise that the appropriate table for the rates in force at the date of death must be used for calculations. In some circumstances, if the deceased person has made substantial lifetime gifts of property within seven years of his death, or longer if he retained an interest in that property, then all or some of the nil rate may not be available. In this case a solicitor must be consulted because tax may also be payable on the previous gifts as well as on the estate at the date of death. A gift of shares in a private company can have complicated tax consequences.

Small gifts and other exemptions
No tax at all is payable on the following gifts:

- *Small presents* – any number of individual gifts of up to £250 per recipient and, apart from these, other gifts totalling up to £3,000 by any donor in each year are wholly exempt in any event. This allowance can be carried forward for one year, if unused.

- *Gifts to a surviving spouse* – all property passing between husband and wife: husband and wife are regarded as entirely separate entities for inheritance tax purposes, but any property which passes from one to the other on the death of one of them is wholly exempt from inheritance tax. This provision does not apply to unmarried partners.

- *Gifts to children in consideration of their marriage*, up to £5,000 per parent.

- *Charities* – all gifts by will to a charity are wholly exempt from inheritance tax.

- *Political parties* – gifts in a will to the main established political parties are exempt.

- *Gifts to the nation or of public benefit* – gifts to certain national museums or collections and some objects or property of national importance, are exempt.

There are also a number of variable exemptions or 'reliefs' affecting such types of property as Lloyd's underwriting accounts, farmland, forestry and timber, partnership businesses and family company shares. It is essential to seek a lawyer's advice if you are involved with any of these: the qualification rules for these reliefs are very complicated and so is the calculation of the figures involved.

Calculation of inheritance tax payable

The following explanations assume that the person who has died ('the deceased') has made no lifetime gifts other than the usual birthday, Christmas and similar 'small' (that is, under £250) gifts and other sums coming to less than £3,000 a year.

Remember that, for the calculations, the scale of rates operative at the date of death must be used.

Harold (H) and Winifred (W) are married. On 1 June 1996 H dies, leaving all his property to his wife W. His total estate is valued at £154,000. The size of his estate is irrelevant because all the property passes to W and is exempt because she is his spouse.

On 1 October 1996 W dies. Her estate is worth £308,000 (she had approximately £154,000 of her own property and also received £154,000 from H's estate when he died). Under her will, all of the property passes equally to their two children Sam (S) and Diana (D), apart from a legacy of £9,000 which was given specifically by W's will to 'The Gentle Home', a registered charity.

On H's death no IHT is payable because of the spouse exemption (it is also below the IHT threshold).

On W's death the calculation is as follows:

£9,000 to charity	– exempt
£200,000 nil rate	– tax payable: nil
£99,000 taxable at 40%	– total tax payable: £39,000

However, there may be scope for saving tax.

Saving tax
If H had died on 1 June 1996 and left all his property to his children S and D, no inheritance tax would have been payable on his £154,000 (he could have left £200,000 without IHT charge).

If W dies on 1 October 1996, leaving her own estate of £154,000 to the children, there will be no tax to pay (unless there has meanwhile been a change in the rates of tax) so that the total tax payable on the joint estates of the husband and wife, which eventually all goes to the children S and D, is nothing rather than £39,600. The reason for this is that the aggregation of the husband's and wife's estates is avoided and therefore the nil-rate tax band in both estates (up to £215,000 in each) is utilised, instead of only one lot of £215,000 nil-rate, when W dies, after all the property has passed from H to W on his death.

In this example W could leave the £9,000 to her children, without incurring any tax.

Sometimes the rates of tax will change between the husband's death and the wife's death, but the same principle applies and the maximum saving is obviously achieved when the nil-rate band has been fully utilised in both estates.

In case of deaths close together
A husband will usually want to make sure his wife benefits from his estate on his death, so that she will have as much property as possible to use for the rest of her life. It is possible, however, for a husband and wife to die in, or as a result of, some joint accident so that one of them survives the other only for a few days or weeks. He or she will have inherited the property without any opportunity of enjoying it.

For that reason a husband and wife may wish to leave their property to the other with the proviso that, in order to inherit, the survivor must survive for at least, say, 30 days. If the survivor dies within that period, the property does not go to the survivor but will pass directly to the children.

The stipulated survival time could be some other number of days; 30 is usually chosen because if the survivor survives for more than 30 days, the chances are that he or she will have some independent life after the deceased and should therefore benefit from the property. This may not necessarily save tax, depending on the relative sizes of the estates. For example, H has an estate of £430,000; W has a nil estate. H's will leaves £215,000 to the children and the residue to W, provided she survives him by 30 days. H and W die in a common accident, W surviving it by (say) 20 days. The whole of H's estate passes to the children and IHT is payable on £215,000 at 40% = £86,600.

Without the survivorship clause, £215,000 would have passed to the children using H's nil-rate band and the residue to W. Using her nil-rate band no IHT would have been payable when her estate passed to the children. However, the decision to include or exclude a survivorship clause must depend on the tax-planning of each person's estate. Advice should be sought where there is a possible liability to IHT.

These 'survivorship' provisions cannot apply where all property is owned as joint tenants between H and W because the property would then become owned automatically by the survivor irrespective of the terms of the will. The joint tenancy would have to be severed, to create a tenancy-in-common, before any share in a co-owned property could be disposed of by will.

Variation within two years of a death

There are some rules which allow the adult beneficiaries of an estate to vary the provisions of the will or the distribution upon an intestacy within a period of two years from the date of the deceased's death, so that the property may pass to them in a more tax-efficient manner than would have been the case had the provisions of the deceased's will been put into operation. These are called deeds of variation or deeds of family arrangement and can enable some post mortem tax-planning to be done.

A variation usually, but not necessarily, operates where beneficiaries of the wills are the same. The important point is that the beneficiaries of the intestacy or the will that is being varied have to enter into the deed of variation as well as the personal representatives.

Anyone considering varying a person's estate to achieve some tax-saving should certainly consult a solicitor to advise on the savings to be achieved, if any, and also to prepare the appropriate documents.

Substantial savings can be achieved, in particular, where the nil-rate band is utilised in both estates. But if a variation is being considered during the life of the surviving spouse, it is most important to make sure that the surviving spouse, W in our example, has enough capital for the rest of her life and to support the children while they are still young.

If the children are not young, and there is a lot of money, it might be possible for both the husband and wife to leave an amount equivalent to the current nil-rate band to their children so that the allowance is utilised in both cases. Bear in mind, however, that if any legacies of money or other items such as gifts under the 'PET' provisions (see page 25) utilise part of the nil-rate band, this will reduce the amount remaining for such a legacy to the children or could lead to tax being paid if the total amount of legacies given is more than £215,000 (or the equivalent nil-rate band at the time). It should also be remembered that the adult beneficiaries cannot legally make any variation that will reduce the entitlement of an infant beneficiary unless it is approved by the court.

The house

A gift to a son or daughter of a parent's own main residence would not be an effective gift for saving inheritance tax if there were any understanding that the giver would be allowed to go on living there, but giving away a house unconditionally, or perhaps a second home where the question of the donor remaining there would not even arise, could lead to considerable tax-saving, depending on the number of years between the gift and the donor's death.

Jointly owned property and tax-saving

There are two forms of joint ownership of a house: joint tenancy and tenancy-in-common. In the case of a joint tenancy, if one of the two co-owners dies, the survivor will become entitled to the house automatically – irrespective of the provisions of the deceased's will (or the rules relating to intestacy). In the case of a tenancy-in-common, the deceased's share of the house will pass under the terms of the will (or in accordance with the rules of intestacy governing the deceased's estate). However, if the property is owned by, say, a mother and her daughter or a cohabiting couple or two friends, liability to IHT will arise if the value of the estate exceeds the IHT threshold, regardless of whether there is a joint tenancy or a tenancy-in-common.

An IHT saving can be effected, using the tenancy-in-common, in circumstances where a married couple is prepared to sever the joint tenancy of the matrimonial home in order to create a tenancy-in-common. Each spouse then makes a will giving his/her half-share in the matrimonial home to the children, thus taking advantage of the tax-exempt allowance of £215,000 on the first death.

Some security can be provided for the surviving spouse by way of a lease for life or by imposing other conditions to protect the surviving spouse but, even so, it is a tricky area, on which legal advice should be sought.

Some other ways of saving inheritance tax

There are other ways in which inheritance tax may be saved, but these are more elaborate and beyond the scope of this book. They are mentioned here so that you can give them consideration, but you should seek the necessary professional advice before you go ahead.

For instance, it is possible to include a complicated provision in a will whereby, for a period of two years from a person's death, the estate is held on trust for a class of people – usually 'my husband/wife and children', or 'my brothers and sisters' – and the executors may, at their discretion, pay out the capital to any member of the class at any time within that period. This is called a 'two-year discretionary trust' and is very flexible because the decision as to who will get what part of the property can be left for up to two years after death, and can therefore be used to obtain efficient inheritance tax treatment of a person's property at death. In this way (even though it may not ultimately be as efficient a distribution of property for inheritance tax purposes as would, for example, leaving it all to the children), the wife can get the capital, or part of it, from the estate if and when she needs it, and the decision to pay it to her can be made at the last moment, thus preserving the possibilities of at least reducing the tax burden.

Deeds of variation and family arrangement (see page 21) which can be entered into within two years of the deceased's death can be made to effect substantial savings of inheritance tax where there are, for example, business assets or Lloyd's underwriting accounts, farming or woodland property or family company shares. Professional advice should always be sought in such cases: the cost of such advice would be small in comparison with the savings likely to be achieved.

The government can reconsider all these rules from time to time and may pass legislation which will severely restrict these possibilities. It is essential, therefore, to take advice before acting.

Inheritance tax on lifetime gifts

In certain circumstances, tax is payable on lifetime gifts (at one-half of the rate which would apply on death). These are fairly unusual, but include gifts by individuals to discretionary trusts in which no other people have an immediate interest in the income, or a gift to a company. On assessing the tax payable for any one particular lifetime gift, you have to look back seven years to see what the total amount of gifts already made immediately prior to the particular gift has been. The matter is complicated and professional advice should be taken before going ahead with such a gift.

Lifetime gifts and their effect on IHT
The basic rule is that no inheritance tax is payable on gifts by one person to another in his or her life, only on death. The situation becomes more complicated, however, when gifts have been made by the deceased person shortly before the end of his life. All gifts within a period of seven years before death have to be aggregated to find a point on the scale at which the tax is payable. If the nil-rate band was used up by the lifetime gift, the executors will have to pay tax on the whole of the estate.

Lifetime exemptions
Gifts up to £3,000 per year are exempt from tax. Any unused part of this can be carried forward for one year, but the current year's annual exemption must always be used before utilising any part of the previous year's allowance carried forward. The allowance can never be carried forward more than one year. Also, small gifts such as birthday presents up to £250 to any one individual in a year are exempt, as are wedding gifts to certain relations, the amount of the exemption depending on the

degree of the relationship (£5,000 per parent or £20,000 in total from both sets of parents, with lesser amounts from other relatives).

The seven-year 'PETS'

The most usual form of lifetime gift which is relevant for inheritance tax is a gift by one person to another. Such a gift is exempt from tax provided the donor lives on for another seven years. Accountants and solicitors call them by the acronym 'PET', which stands for 'potentially exempt transfer' (although, strictly speaking, it is a potentially chargeable transfer).

If such a lifetime gift is made without strings attached and the donor survives for seven years, there can be no possibility of tax being charged. But if a donor makes a gift and does not survive for seven years, tax may be payable on that gift if it exceeds the nil-rate band. The tax will, however, be at a reduced percentage, depending on the number of years that have elapsed between the date of the gift and the date of death. Thus:

- on a death within 3 years of a taxable gift 100% of the death rate tax is payable
- on a death between 3 and 4 years after the taxable gift, 80% is payable
- on a death between 4 and 5 years, 60%
- on a death between 5 and 6 years, 40%
- on a death between 6 and 7 years, 20%
- on a death more than 7 years after the gift, no inheritance tax is payable.

(Under the old capital transfer tax rules, CTT was payable at the full death rates for a lifetime gift within three years of the date of death; for lifetime gifts more than three years before the date of death, tax was payable at only 50% of the rate payable on death.)

The gift may also affect the rates at which tax is payable on the donor's estate when he dies because the amount is counted in with the rest of the estate. The point on the inheritance tax scale at which the tax is calculated is assessed by looking at the total amount of chargeable lifetime gifts made by the deceased person in the seven years prior to the date of death, minus any amount of exempt gifts.

EXAMPLE

For the purpose of the example, it is assumed that the rates of inheritance tax will remain the same throughout (although they can be changed as the Chancellor directs). Neither is consideration given to the complexities of the rules in relation to business assets, agricultural property, timber and the like, for which professional advice must be sought.

In June 1995 G makes a gift of £2,000 to his son S. This is wholly exempt, being under the £3,000 annual limit.

In June 1996 G makes a gift of £1,750 to each of his daughters D and E, so that the total gift in the tax year 6 April 1996 to 5 April 1997 is £3,500. £3,000 is exempt under the annual exemption for that year. The rest is exempt because there was £1,000 of unused annual exemption to bring forward from the previous year. £500 of that annual exemption from the previous year is not utilised, but cannot be carried forward to the following year because of the rule that the unused annual exemption can be carried forward for one year only and the current year's annual exemption must always be used first.

In June 1997 G makes other gifts as follows. He gives to S and D £100,000 each and to E he gives his second home, a cottage in the country worth £100,000.

The total gift is therefore £300,000. Of this, £3,000 is exempt under the annual exemption. None of the remainder (£297,000) is taxable under inheritance tax rules which abolished tax on certain lifetime gifts. However, the gifts could become taxable if G died within seven years, depending on the value of his estate. S, D and E could therefore find that on G's death they receive a demand for inheritance tax payable on the gifts they have received. (They should therefore either set aside a sum to cover this, or take out insurance to provide an amount to cover the tax payable on G's possible death within seven years. A 'decreasing term' insurance would be suitable, in which the premiums are averaged out to be the same throughout, but the sum insured gets smaller in step with the decrease in the size of the potential tax bill.)

If G does die within seven years, tax could be payable on the gifts he made in June 1997, assessed at the rates shown by the inheritance tax table that is current at the date of G's death.

G fails to survive for seven years: he dies in May 2002. Since the gifts in June 1997, he has made no more taxable gifts (only some wholly exempt ones within the annual allowance or usual presents).

His estate is worth £300,000. In his will, he gives to his wife (W) his main house which is worth £80,000 and is in his sole name, and he also gives her a legacy of £80,000. He directs that the rest of his property should go to each of his three children equally.

The tax payable is calculated on the lifetime gifts and on the estate as follows.

On the lifetime gifts to the children
Tax payable at 'death rates' (that is, inheritance tax rates) on the chargeable gifts of £297,000 is:

on the first £215,000, – nil
on the balance of £82,000 at 40% – £32,800

However, death occurred between four and five years after the original gifts, so tax is reduced to 60% of the death rates. Therefore the total tax in relation to lifetime gifts is £19,680 and S, D and E will each have to pay £6,560 inheritance tax.

On the estate of G
The legacies to W (totalling £160,000) are exempt because there is no inheritance tax on property passing between husband and wife.

The taxable estate is therefore £140,000, which is the residue passing to the three children equally. In the last seven years, the only chargeable gifts made by G were those of June 1997 (which came to £297,000). Therefore the point on the inheritance tax table at which to start the calculation on the estate is £140,000 at 40%, the nil-rate band of tax having been used up by the lifetime gifts to the children.

Tax payable on £140,000 at 40% is £56,000 and the total tax payable is therefore £56,000 on the estate (plus that of £19,680 to be paid by the children on their gifts).

In the example, we have assumed that the tax rates remain constant for the whole period. It is most likely that new figures will be published each year, and when dealing with the lifetime gifts it is the table current at the date of death that is used to calculate the tax. But the value of the property given during the donor's life is assessed as at the date of the original gift, even if it has meanwhile gone up in value, as may be the case with a house, or has earned any income. This in itself could result in a large saving of inheritance tax if assets which are anticipated to go up in value are chosen.

So there is an advantage in giving property away even if it turns out that the gift was made within three years of the donor's death, if the property is likely to increase in value with the years. If the gift is not cash, it is wise to have the property or item valued at the date of the gift, in case the value is disputed later.

Joint property

Where a property is jointly owned, any inheritance tax is assessed by reference only to the person who actually receives the deceased's interest in the property. It makes no difference who is the co-owner or whether the property was held as tenants-in-common or joint tenants. If the share of the house passes to the spouse (whether by the will or by virtue of a joint tenancy), this will be exempt from inheritance tax. But if it passes to any taxable beneficiary (for example, boyfriend/girlfriend or son, daughter or parent), then it will be taxable.

What should be foreseen

Lifetime gifts give considerable scope for passing property or money and so on from one generation to another, without paying tax, but the donor does need to survive for seven years for the full advantages to be gained. When considering whether or not to give away property in your lifetime, you must always have due regard to the property which you require for the rest of your life, and also try to make sure that your husband or wife will be adequately provided for. Many problems are caused because people wish to save tax and therefore give away all their property to their children, and hope that the children will 'do the right thing'. Even in the most close-knit of families, the fact that a spouse knows that he or she has to rely on the goodwill of the children can create a certain amount of ill-feeling and mistrust.

Who gets the residue?

In the example, the wife was given a particular sum of money and the house by G's will, and the children were given the residue of the estate. What would have been the position if the children had been given a legacy and the wife had been given the residue of the estate? This is in fact more usual, but the calculations required are much more complicated. This is because the wife's entitlement to the residue can be calculated only after the tax has been calculated on the gift to the children.

Who pays the tax?

In our example, if G had given the sum of £140,000 to be divided equally between his children 'subject to the payment of all taxes and duties by reference to my death' on that amount of the legacy, the calculation would have been exactly the same. It is more usual that a legacy is given 'free of all taxes and duties payable on or by reference to my death' (and this is implied if it is not specified in the will). This means that the children would have to receive £140,000 after the tax has been calculated. But the tax rules state that the tax payable on the legacy counts as part of the legacy itself, for tax purposes. This means that one would have to gross up the legacy of £140,000 and the question therefore becomes: 'what total amount of taxable legacy will leave £140,000 after the tax on that legacy has been paid?' The Inland Revenue publish 'grossing-up' tables, from which the answer can be calculated. In G's particular case, the amount of legacy to be given to the three children between them which would leave them £140,000 after the tax had been paid would be approximately £234,000. This would have left his widow with only something like £66,000.

It is therefore very important, from the inheritance tax point of view, if there have been taxable gifts of amounts exceeding the nil-rate band of inheritance tax within (what may turn out to be) the last seven years before death, that the widow should be given an absolute legacy rather than a share in residue, and that the children's interest should be a share in residue and not a legacy.

The alternative is to say in the will that any legacy given to the children must bear its own tax. In this way, the person making the will knows that the amount by which the estate will be decreased by the legacy is limited to the amount specified, and will not need to be 'grossed up' for inheritance tax purposes, so that the amount which the widow will receive from the estate will not be put at risk, even if the net amount of the other legacies will be decreased. Another option would be to limit the children's legacy to the amount that could be given without IHT becoming chargeable.

What cannot be foreseen

The best opportunity for saving inheritance tax really arises when a husband and wife die within two years of each other so that the estate of the first one to die can be varied by means of a deed of variation (see page 21) between the beneficiaries of both parents' estates. The question of adequate provision for the survivor (who has already died within the two-year period) does not have to be considered and maximum tax-saving can be achieved.

If at any time you make a gift but reserve an interest, such as a right to reside in the gifted house, your gift will be taken into account and the value will be the value of the property at the date of your death.

CHAPTER 2

MAKING A WILL

ANYONE can make a will provided he or she is at least 18 years old and of sound mind. Being of sound mind means that the testator must appreciate the nature of the document he is signing, and its effect. If there is a dispute later, medical evidence is admitted, if necessary, to show that this was the case (or not) at the time the will was made. The will can therefore be made and signed in a lucid period during a psychiatric illness, although you may find that some hospitals and old people's homes have rules preventing nurses from witnessing the wills of patients.

The contents of your will

A will usually has three distinct sections. The first deals with the appointment of executors (the people responsible for dealing with all your affairs after your death) and any guardians for children, funeral wishes and similar preliminary matters.

The second section deals with the distribution of your property – that is, who is to have what after your death.

The third section contains any powers that the executors will need in order to carry out their duties properly.

So, before you can start to write your will, you have to decide many important issues.

Choosing your executors

Executors are always appointed by will. If a will does not appoint any executors, your next of kin will usually be the people responsible for administering your estate; they are then called administrators. Executors and administrators are a form of trustee. Executors have power to deal with the affairs of the testator (the person making the will) from the moment of his death, but administrators have no such authority, and must theoretically wait for the court to grant letters of administration before taking any action at all. This can present great problems if there is a dispute about who is to make the funeral arrangements, or if certain members of the family start going through the possessions of the deceased.

Trustees

Trustees are simply persons who legally own and administer property but are not usually allowed to benefit themselves from that property. They have to manage the property for the benefit of other people, the beneficiaries. For example, a trust arises where property is given to children under the age of 18, and trustees then hold the property for the benefit of the children until they reach the age of 18. The terms on which the property is held in trust is provided for them either in the document setting up the trust (which can be a will) or in various Acts of Parliament.

An executor is a special kind of trustee because he is responsible for administering all the affairs of the testator when he dies. He is also in a unique position because, if the will specifies, he is allowed to receive a benefit by way of legacy from the estate, even though he is an executor or trustee of the property.

One major difference between executors and trustees is that ordinary trustees can be dismissed by the people having any beneficial interest in the property, provided they all agree. But an executor, so long as he is not guilty of any misconduct, cannot be forced to renounce or retire. It could therefore be difficult to persuade a bank, for example, that it is not required to act, if one or more members of the family are joint executors with the bank and could act quite satisfactorily without the bank.

Once the administration of an estate has been completed, by realising the assets, paying the debts and distributing the residue, the executors' job is finished. They may, however, continue to work as trustees if, for instance, some of the money has to be held for minors until they reach 18.

What executors do

The executors' duties are no mere formalities: there is a great deal of work involved and much responsibility. They will be responsible first for collecting in all the assets of the estate and drawing up all the lists of property, dealing with the paperwork and calculations, paying all the debts, liabilities and taxes and the various costs such as funeral costs and administration costs, and then ultimately for dealing with all the property that remains in the estate in accordance with the terms of the will. They may have to pay legacies of money to nominated persons, transfer particular items of property to a beneficiary, pay out the estate to one or more specified beneficiaries, or hold the property 'in trust' on the terms specified in the testator's will.

Whom to appoint

You cannot force someone to take on the duties of being your executor, so it is much better to ask the people you have in mind first if they agree to be appointed. An executor may not really wish to act but will feel duty bound to do so when the time comes, because he has been appointed. You should therefore try to find someone whom you know will be willing to act.

In normal circumstances, a husband will appoint his wife to be his executor, and vice versa, especially where they do not have grown-up children. This is a good idea, as a rule, because the wife/husband will usually be receiving most of the estate. It is sensible that the person who has the biggest stake in the estate should have a hand in its administration.

It is perhaps as well, though, that a wife (or husband) should not be the only executor. She will have enough to cope with at the time of her husband's death without this – and there may, of course, be some common accident. Whom to choose as the other executor should depend largely on the circumstances of the people concerned. If there are infant children, it may be sensible to have a professional person, for example a solicitor or an accountant, to act because the property will subsequently have to be held in trust for the children, although there is no reason why it should not be a trusted friend of the family. If the children have attained their majority, one or other of the children can be a joint executor. Often, the grown-up children are executors and the spouse is not.

It is common to appoint two executors. This is a good idea where the burden needs to be shared, and it is virtually essential where the will would set up a trust, for example for children. If the executor is not a member of the immediate family, and not someone who is a professional, and is therefore undertaking the duties as a trusted friend, it is sometimes thought suitable to leave him a legacy – £250, say – for undertaking the office of executor. Otherwise, executors are entitled to recover only their expenses.

When a solicitor is appointed to be an executor, the solicitor will include a clause in your will enabling him to charge normal professional fees for his legal work in administering the estate. Without a charging clause, as it is called, he would not be entitled to a fee. But usually he would not be given any specific legacy of money, unless he was also a special personal friend.

Appointing a bank

A bank can act as an executor of your will. You may consider appointing a bank as an executor if there is no one individual to whom you feel you could entrust this task, maybe because there are family arguments. However, the disadvantages of having a bank as an executor include the fact that the costs of administration of the estate will be considerably more than those of professional trustees and executors, such as accountants and solicitors. Also, banks do not always have the personal knowledge of the family that an individual appointed by you would usually have. There are likely to be some tasks which require a personal touch, such as sorting out the personal belongings of the person who has died, for instance. Banks may employ competent and sympathetic staff, but they are no substitute for the right friend or relation.

Sometimes a bank is appointed to be an executor jointly with an individual, perhaps a member of the family or a close friend.

When the time comes to consider administering the estate, the individual executor may feel quite capable of doing so himself without the assistance of the bank, but if the estate is large it is very unlikely that the bank would agree to renounce its role and therefore its fee. If you are going to appoint a bank to be your executor, you should, in the will, use the appointment clause supplied by the bank.

If you are considering appointing any commercial organisation, including a bank, to be your executor, look carefully at its own literature and publicity and in particular the rates of charging for administering the estate, including such things as acceptance fees, arrangement fees, annual management fees and withdrawal fees. Work out how much it will cost, especially if the administration is likely to be straightforward. If you are leaving everything to your wife and adult children, it may not be necessary to use them at all.

The Public Trustee is a government department which can be appointed to be your executor, as can some trust corporations. These all operate in much the same way as a bank acting as executor, and charge for this service. (There is, however, no such service in Northern Ireland.)

In addition to the bank's and Public Trustee's own charges for administering the estate, there will also be solicitors' fees for the probate work.

All in all, it is probably better to appoint individuals to be your executors, if suitable candidates are willing to act, and it is usually preferable to select as an executor a person who is younger than you. It is also sensible to provide in your will for a substitute executor to act if one or other (or both) of those appointed should die before you, or not wish to act as your executor.

Guardians

You can state in your will whom you wish to take on the obligations and liabilities of bringing up your children rather than leaving it to the court to decide who is the most suitable person. For anyone with young children, it is sensible to appoint a guardian (or guardians). Under the provisions of the Children Act 1989, a person must have parental responsibility before he can appoint a guardian for a child. The father of an illegitimate child could not appoint a guardian unless he already had parental responsibility. If he has got parental responsibility, he should seek legal advice if he wishes to make a will appointing a guardian.

If either a father or mother dies, the survivor will usually be responsible for bringing up the children. However, on the death of the survivor or following some common accident in which the husband and wife die within a short time of each other, the appointment of guardians will become effective. Generally, guardianship would arise only after the death of both parents.

The choice of guardians requires very careful consideration as to the personal qualities of the friends by whom you wish your children to be brought up, and also their discernment in financial matters. The guardians will obviously wish to know that funds will be available for the maintenance of the children, otherwise they would probably not be able to afford to take on the liabilities. If the appointment of guardians takes effect, the estate will almost always be held in trust for the children. It is obviously a good idea, therefore, to make the guardians executors and trustees. It is, however, not necessarily the best thing that they should be the only executors and trustees. Perhaps a professional trustee (for example, a solicitor) should join them as trustee, to give an independent view of how the property is dealt with. He can also help with the formalities of the administration and investment of the money, if the guardians will be absorbed in the day-to-day upbringing of the children.

Who should inherit?

Before deciding whom you wish to benefit from your will, it is a good idea to set down a rough calculation of your estate and what it is worth. You need not be too exact about this because it is bound to change by the time you die. The assets you have at present will change in value, you will acquire new ones and dispose of some of those that you have, and there will also be debts and liabilities and mortgages and such things, all of which can alter between the time you make your will and when you die. Nevertheless, it is a good idea to know roughly how much your estate is worth and, if you are married, consider this also with your spouse, so that you can make an assessment of what the tax payable will be if you benefit various particular people. Do not forget any lifetime gifts.

When drawing up the list of assets, remember to deduct from the value of the house the mortgage which is outstanding, unless this is covered by a mortgage protection policy or an endowment insurance policy so that the mortgage would automatically be repaid on your death. Remember also any other benefits which are payable on your death by reason of other life policies or pension fund payments, your car, and all of the possessions in your house.

Then make a note of the people to whom you wish to give any legacies, possibly a friend who has agreed to act as executor; list any particular items you want to leave to special people, for example your wedding ring to your granddaughter, or the piano to your nephew. If the gifts are valuable, make a note of their likely value. You may wish to give money to a few of your friends, relations, godchildren or people who have been particularly helpful to you in some way or other (for example, £100 to the child of an old friend).

You can also give a sum of money to a class of people, for example '£500 to each of my brothers and sisters living at my death' or one particular sum of money, for example '£2,000 to be divided equally between all my grandchildren living at my death'. Avoid gifts to a class of people which may not be known for many years, e.g. 'to all my grandchildren'. You may have a son aged 30 who fathers a child when he is 60. If you died soon after making your will, your executors would have to wait at least 30 years to be sure that all the grandchildren had been born. It is important to specify carefully the class of people whom you wish to benefit and to specify, for example, whether it includes illegitimate children and whether your husband's brother's sons are covered by the word 'nephew'. (For these purposes, there is now no legal distinction between children born in wedlock and adopted children.) Are the husbands of aunts included in the word 'uncles', or does it mean brothers of parents only? Does it include illegitimate nephews? If there is any doubt at all, it is better to list the people by their names.

Remember that the will is operative only from the date of your death. If you leave someone a particular item of jewellery or any other piece of property and you dispose of it before your death, the beneficiary will not receive that item of property.

You may wish to give a sum to a charity. Often, people leave a sum of money to a particular charity with which they have been concerned in their life, for one reason or another. A particular friend or relative may have benefited from a heart research foundation or leukaemia fund, for example, and so you might wish to make a donation to that particular charity. It is very important to get the name and address of the charity correct, otherwise the gift could be invalidated. It is also wise to give an alternative in case the charity no longer exists at the date of your death.

The rest of your estate

It is impossible to specify the amount of money which will go to the residuary beneficiary. Even if this could be calculated at today's date, it would certainly not operate on your death any number of months or years hence. All you can do, therefore, is to specify who is to receive the rest of your estate. The lawyers call it 'residue'; the term 'residuary estate' is everything that is left after all the debts, liabilities, taxes, costs and legacies have been paid or transferred. The residue can go to one person, or to a number of people in equal or unequal shares.

Life interest or absolute gift

You then have to decide if you wish the main beneficiaries of your estate to have the property (meaning the capital of your estate) outright (or 'absolutely'), that is, without any condition whatsoever. Or do you wish them to have an interest for the rest of their life only, so that the property will then pass to someone you have chosen, rather than in accordance with the will (or intestacy) of the first beneficiary? If this is the case, bear in mind that the first beneficiary will be able to use only the income from the property during his (or her) life. He will be entitled to the interest and/or dividends on the money or investments, and be able to have the use of any property which does not earn income, such as the house or contents of the house. It would be possible to rent out the house and receive the rent. (There can be complications as to repair, maintenance and outgoings of a house where the interest is limited in this way, and it may be wise to consult a solicitor on how to state the situation clearly in the will. The right wording is extremely important as you may establish a right to reside in a house or a life interest with very different consequences.) After your death, during the life of the beneficiary, there will be certain costs of administering the estate, completing income tax returns and trust accounts, so a professional executor should perhaps be appointed.

If you have provided that the residue should be invested and only the income paid to someone (your wife, perhaps, during her life), the capital itself would have to be divided between other people (your children, perhaps) on the death of the life tenant (that is, the person entitled to the income for life). This means that the property will, on that person's death, devolve in accordance with your own will and not under the will of (or intestacy relating to) the life tenant's estate, which would have been the case had the property been given outright. Legal advice is essential if you are considering giving someone a life interest in your estate. These matters can be important where, for instance, you wish to guarantee that the property is kept in your family rather than allowing it to pass to your wife's family. It may be even more relevant where, for example, you have children from a previous marriage or if you are living with a partner to whom you are not married and you wish her or him to be provided for, for life, but also to guarantee that any of your children benefit from your property after the death of your present partner.

Usually, however, most people will wish to give the property outright, that is, make an absolute gift.

Trying to disinherit a dependant
When deciding who should benefit, most people naturally favour the members of their own immediate family, and this is a notion which the law encourages. Although you are free to give all of your assets to anyone you state in your will, certain

people who are closely related to you in one way or another and whom you have supported can, regardless of the terms of your will, make an application to the court for a share in your estate. If for any reason you decide that your spouse or any of your children or anyone else financially dependent on you should inherit little or nothing under your will, after your death any of them might apply to the executors, or to the court, for reasonable provision to be made for them out of what you left. The same rules apply if someone has been left out because of the intestacy rules (a cohabitee, for example).

Those who can apply for some provision to be made in this way are:

- the surviving husband or wife
- a former wife or husband who has not remarried (unless this right has been excluded as part of the divorce settlement)
- sons or daughters (including stepchildren) regardless of their age
- anyone who has been maintained by you before you died
- a cohabitee.

You cannot therefore guarantee that these people will not benefit from your estate. The application has to be made within six months of the Grant of Probate or Letters of Administration.

There are circumstances where such people can properly be excluded from benefiting from your estate, for example because a wife has already been given a house and large sum during the husband's lifetime, or is financially wholly independent. But to ensure that the best wording for this is used in your will, you should take professional advice in such circumstances.

Beneficiary dying first

If a son or daughter of yours, destined to receive something under your will, dies before you, but a child or grandchild of that son or daughter survives you, the gift you had intended to leave to the son or daughter will go to that son's or daughter's issue unless you make specific provision that it should not do so.

In any other case the gift will fail on the death of the beneficiary unless you make a specific provision for his or her children to receive the gift instead. In a case of a pecuniary legacy ('£100 to John Brown') or a specific bequest ('my diamond brooch to Jane Brown') no problem arises – if John Brown, or Jane Brown, is dead, the gift will simply become part of the residue and swell the amount that will go to the person who is to receive the residuary estate.

If the residuary beneficiary himself dies first, that would leave part of your property undisposed of – this is called a partial intestacy. It is wise to provide for an alternative if your will provides for only one residuary beneficiary.

The important factor is who was alive at the date of death. It does not matter whether a beneficiary dies before actually receiving the benefit from the estate. For example, if a friend is given a legacy of £250 in a will, but dies after the testator but before the £250 is actually paid to him, the beneficiary's estate will receive that money; it does not go into the residuary estate of the original testator.

Husband and wife
Generally, a husband gives the main part of his estate to his wife, so that the wife becomes the residuary beneficiary. If the wife were to die first, the husband could make a fresh will, making provision for the children instead; if there are no children, he could dispose of his estate elsewhere, according to the circumstances.

But it might happen that husband and wife are both victims of the same road accident, the wife being killed outright and the husband surviving for a few days, but then dying without having had a chance to make a new will. In this case the husband's intention of leaving everything to his wife would be largely defeated because she would have died first. What then happens to the bulk of his property, which his will left to her, follows the rules of intestacy. These might well not accord with his wishes. It would therefore be better for the husband to make specific provision for this possibility in the will itself, by saying to whom his property should go if his wife does not survive him (and, similarly, a wife in her will). In many cases, this would be the children. If they are under age, the will might go on to deal with that situation in greater detail, for instance, to lift some of the restrictions that would otherwise limit the executors' powers of investing the property for the children's benefit, and similar matters.

To cover the case of such a joint accident in which it is impossible to know who will survive whom and by how long, a will can contain a provision that the wife (or husband) will inherit the property provided that she or he survives for a given number of days and, if that does not happen, the will specifies who should benefit. Be careful of the IHT consequences if you include such a clause in your will.

If a person who has not made a will dies on or after 1 January 1996 a surviving spouse will inherit only if he or she survives by 28 days.

In Scotland, if husband and wife both die and it cannot be ascertained who died first, neither is deemed to have survived the other.

CHAPTER 3

WHAT TO SAY IN A WILL

A WILL is chiefly concerned with disposing of assets, but it can be used for incidental matters as well. Perhaps the commonest of these, traditionally, is to specify the way in which you want your body to be disposed of – burial or cremation. It is more important to let your nearest relative or the person you live with know than to put it in your will. Consumers' Association's *What to Do When Someone Dies* gives details of what to do if you wish to leave your body for medical education or research.

A will is not the place for philosophical reflection, nor for expressing love, gratitude, hate, despair or any feeling about the world in general, or anyone in particular. When you are dead, your will will eventually be available as a public document, and anyone can then apply to see it at Somerset House and also obtain a copy of it.

You may not want your private thoughts to be open to the public gaze. It is possible to leave something to someone whose name you do not wish to appear on your will, by setting up a 'secret' or 'half-secret' trust. For this, it is essential that you seek a lawyer's advice.

Do not put down any outrageous thoughts or reasons for making particular gifts or failing to leave anything to, for example, a close relative. A will can be invalid if the testator is insane or if it can be shown that he did not give proper consideration to those obligations he ought to have considered.

Say it simply and clearly

You should aim to be precise and clear in what you say in your will. Express your wishes simply, without embellishment, explanation or apology. If you really want to make it clear why you have left your property as you have, it is probably better to do this in an ordinary letter which can be left with the will. It is always possible that if you were to go into unnecessary detail in the will itself, you might unwittingly affect the interpretation that would be put on the words. For example, if you were to say 'I give £500 to my cousin Willie Bolter, confident that he will do what is right by the rest of my cousins' the question might arise whether this created a binding legal trust in favour of the other cousins or whether Willie Bolter could take the £500 himself. Instead, say either 'I give £500 to my cousin Willie Bolter' and leave it at that, or 'I give £500 to be divided equally between ...'.

It is also inadvisable to say 'I leave £500 to Mr and Mrs Harry Green' because this does not make it clear whether they should receive £500 each or £500 between them, or what is to happen if either one of them were to die before the testator, or if they divorce or remarry.

Never assume that people will know what you mean; they may not, and anyway the will can be interpreted only on the basis of the words you actually use. The rules of interpretation are very strict. Where a testator said one thing in his will, although it is obvious that he meant something different, the law may well stick to what he said, rather than what he meant.

It is easy to cause havoc by choosing inappropriate legal expressions and quite possible to make a will, in a normal case, without using technical language. So, wherever it is possible, avoid legal terminology, even if you think you know the correct legal meaning, and use an ordinary word rather than a legal one. There is a strong case for cutting out a lot of the legal jargon lawyers often employ in drawing up wills for their clients.

At the same time, choose your ordinary language with care. Beware of sloppy loose expressions. If you were to say, 'I give all my money to my wife Clara', this might mean just the cash about the house, or it might mean all the cash plus what is in the bank, or it might mean everything you own. If you intend the latter, you should say, 'I give everything I own to my wife Clara'. To make sure that there are no conditions or strings attached, you can add the word 'absolutely'.

Do not unintentionally create a life interest

A clause in a home-made will which reads like this: 'I leave everything to my wife Clara; and on her death it is to be shared between my sons Albert and Sidney' is a disaster, and likely to have an effect quite different from what the testator intended. The point is this: if he leaves everything to his wife Clara so that, on his death, his assets become her assets, his will cannot then go on to say what is to happen to her assets on her death (or during her lifetime, for that matter). That is for her to deal with, in making her will. She may or may not choose to leave them to the sons Albert and Sidney. If the husband does say what is to happen to them, or what remains of them on her death, the chances are that this leaves his wife with a mere life interest, that is, the right to receive only the income from the assets for the rest of her life, with no right to touch the capital.

If the husband intends that his widow should be able to do what she likes with the capital, and does not intend to restrict her to having only a life interest, he should just say, 'I give everything I own to my wife Clara', and leave her to decide what is to happen to what remains of it by the time she dies.

Revocation clauses

There is one clause which should always be included in a will, namely one saying that any previous wills are revoked. A later will does not automatically revoke an earlier one. If a person leaves two wills, and parts of them are not inconsistent with each other, they stand together; where the wills are inconsistent, the later one prevails. But having two wills is almost always likely to cause problems.

Even though you have not in fact made a will before, it is a good idea to include a statement that previous wills are revoked. Your executors might wonder, after your death, whether perhaps you left any earlier wills. Having a revocation clause in your will saves your executors a fruitless search for any earlier will, by showing that it is revoked anyway.

Here follow some examples of wills in different circumstances, some of which may be like your own.

A. Will of a husband with young children

Matthew Seaton is in his thirties, married with two children, a boy aged six and a girl aged four. He owns his house, which is in his sole name, but he has a mortgage on it with a building society. He has an endowment assurance policy which he hopes will produce £30,000 plus profits in 22 years; this sum is guaranteed on the death of either himself or his wife before that time. He has about £2,000 invested in a building society and the furniture and effects in the house, which belong jointly to himself and his wife, total about £12,000, and he owns his own car valued at approximately £3,000. He has a bank account which is seldom in credit to the tune of more than £150. His salary is £20,000 per year and he hopes to be earning about £25,000 before he reaches his ceiling. His employers run a contributory pension scheme under which he will get a pension when he retires, and under which his wife Emma will receive a pension on his death, and something extra for the children if he dies while they are under 18.

Matthew is in good health and expects to live well into old age but, like anyone else, he may be dead by midnight tonight, so he is making a will. First he makes some notes which he will be sure to destroy once the will is made, in case they might be confused with the will itself. They read like this:

What I own

(1)	House: 14 Twintree Avenue, value say £100,000 Subject to mortgage to Forthright Building Society still owing (about) £30,000, therefore net value of house	£ 70,000
(2)	Endowment life assurance policy worth on death at least	£ 32,000
(3)	Minford Building Society	£ 2,000
(4)	One-half of the value of furniture and effects in the house, say £12,000	£6,000
(5)	Car	£3,000
(6)	Current account at bank, say	£ 200
		£113,200
	call it	£115,000

Notes for will

(1) Revoke previous wills
(2) Executors: Emma and brother David
    substitute for either of them: friend Andrew Shervington
(3) Guardians: Janet and Nicholas
(4) Cremation, eyes and organ transplant
(5) Bequests:
    (i) golf clubs to Donald
    (ii) cello to Daniel
    (iii) lawnmower to Rosemary
(6) Legacies:
    (i) £250 to David or Andrew, if they are my executors
    (ii) £60 to Leslie Roberts
    (iii) £100 to cancer research
(7) Residue to Emma
(8) If she dies before me, trusts for children with appropriate clauses.

Having carefully thought out how he would like to frame his will, Matthew turned his attention to the precise wording. He wrote it out in draft form first, made a few amendments to tidy up the wording and deleted all the commas, except in addresses. Lawyers omit all commas to guard against fraud: a comma can alter the meaning of a sentence and is easier to slip in than extra words, figures or phrases. In a will that was obviously written without any commas, it should then arouse suspicion if one comma were to appear.

Then he typed out the will itself (the engrossment, as lawyers call it) on a large piece of paper. He could have written it out by hand, but word-processing or typing is better, so that there can be no question of illegibility.

He used single spacing, mainly because the whole will would then fit on to both sides of one sheet of paper, leaving sufficient room at the bottom for the signatures of himself and the witnesses. Apart from looking slightly absurd, there could be legal problems if the signatures appeared on a page by themselves. If a will extends to more than one side of a piece of paper, it is best to leave at least one full clause for the next page. Also, the continuation should be on the back of the first page rather than on a fresh sheet.

Matthew was very careful in typing out the will but still made a couple of typing errors. He therefore had to start all over again, and this time managed to avoid making any mistakes.

This is important, because alterations appearing in a will are assumed (unless the contrary is proved) to have been made after the will was signed, and so to form no part of it. If there had been any errors in preparing the engrossment, he and the witnesses would have had to authenticate the alterations by writing their initials in the margin beside each alteration.

This is what he typed:

This will is made by me Matthew John Seaton of 14 Twintree Avenue, Minford, Surrey

1. I revoke all earlier wills and codicils.
2. (a) I appoint as my executors and trustees my wife Emma and my brother David Gordon Seaton.
    (b) If my wife Emma or my brother David are unwilling or unable to act I appoint Andrew Shervington in their place.
3. If my wife Emma dies before me or does not survive me for thirty days then I appoint Janet and Nicholas Saunders to be the guardians of my infant children.
4. (a) I wish my eyes and other parts of my body to be used immediately for medical purposes and subsequently by [institution] and I have made arrangements for this with the appropriate authority.
    (b) I wish the remains of my body to be cremated.
5. I give the following items free from all taxes:
    (a) to my nephew Donald Millington of 16 Durham Terrace, Leeds my golf clubs and bag and trolley
    (b) to my son Daniel my cello
    (c) to my neighbour Rosemary Bruton [address] my mowing machine.
6. I give the following legacies free from all taxes:
    (a) to my brother David the sum of £250 if he proves my will
    (b) to my friend Andrew Shervington the sum of £250 if he proves my will
    (c) to Leslie Roberts of 36 Grove Park, Norwich, the sum of £60 but if he dies before me I leave £60 to his son Andy
    (d) to the Imperial Cancer Research Fund of [address] the sum of £100 and the receipt of a person who appears to be a proper officer of the Charity shall be a discharge to my trustees.
7. I give to my wife Emma the whole of the rest of my estate if she survives me for a period of thirty days.
8. If my wife Emma dies before me or does not survive me for the period of thirty days then the following shall apply:
    (i) I give the whole of the rest of my estate to my executors as trustees. They are to sell everything not in the form of cash but they may postpone the sale of anything as long as they like. After paying my debts and taxes and duties payable on my death and the expense of my funeral and of administering my estate they are to invest or apply what is left.
    (ii) My trustees are to divide whatever is left of my estate (including any income from it) equally between those of my children who

reach the age of eighteen and may apply the actual assets rather than cash if they think fit without requiring the consent of any other person.

(iii) If any child of mine predeceases me or dies under the age of eighteen leaving children who do reach that age then those grandchildren of mine are to divide equally between them the share of my estate which their parent would have received if that parent had lived long enough.

9. My trustees shall have the following powers:

(i) To pay income to which a beneficiary who is under eighteen is entitled to his guardian for his benefit or to the beneficiary upon reaching sixteen.

(ii) To apply capital for the benefit of any beneficiary who is under eighteen as if the Trustee Act 1925 section 32 applied to the whole (and not just half) of the beneficiary's interest in that capital.

(iii) If the house of the guardians of my children is too small to accommodate their family and my children my trustees may lend money to the guardians in order to improve the house or to purchase a new house upon terms which in the opinion of the trustees will not cause the guardians to lose money.

(iv) To invest as freely as if they were beneficially entitled.

Signed by Matthew John Seaton on the [date] 1997 ....
In our presence and attested by us in his presence:

Witness 1: signature ....
address ....
....
occupation ....

Witness 2: signature ....
address ....
....
occupation ....

Matthew Seaton's will was ready to be signed. It would not all fit on to the front of the paper that Matthew was using so he carried over to the back of the sheet, at the point where the will said, '7. I give to my wife Emma ...'.

Comments on Matthew Seaton's will

It is important to make it clear that the document is a will.

Clause 1 Remember that the will takes effect only on your death, so that you can revoke it at any time before then. It is possible to amend a will by executing a codicil without revoking the will in full. It is important to revoke any previous will, and codicil, so that there can be no confusion about the provisions which govern your estate on your death.

Clause 2 The main beneficiary (in Matthew's case, his wife) is appointed to be an executor. Quite apart from saying what should happen if she did not survive, he decides to appoint a substitute executor, in case the appointed co-executor (his brother) is unable or unwilling to assist her with the administration of the estate when the time comes. Any executor can renounce the appointment although no one, not even a spouse or other co-executor, can force another executor to renounce.

Clause 3 In case Emma does not survive Matthew for at least 30 days, he appoints another executor to act with his brother. Sometimes the 'third' executor in a case like this will be a solicitor or accountant. The guardians may certainly be executors, but it is a good idea also to have one independent person to be an executor – otherwise, there is no check on the use of money by the guardians who may be too personally involved in bringing up the children to make proper decisions regarding investments and payment of money.

Clause 4 (a) and (b) A transplant operation can save another person's life, and organs such as heart, liver, kidneys and corneas (to prevent blindness) are always urgently needed. Anyone who has indicated his willingness to be a donor in writing (perhaps by signing a donor card) does not need to repeat it in the will. Making sure that your relatives know, so that they will act swiftly, is more important. If you wish your body to be used for medical research, you should contact the professor of anatomy at your nearest medical school or HM Inspector of Anatomy at the Department of Health.*

Clause 5 It may seem far-fetched that there might be taxes arising on a set of golf clubs. Where inheritance tax is payable, it is usual for this to be paid out of the amount going to the residuary legatee (the person who receives the bulk of the estate). The law automatically implies this, but a change in the law is always possible between the date of the will and death. The phrase 'free from all taxes ...' also avoids complications if there have been sizeable gifts by the testator in the seven years immediately prior to death, using up the nil-rate tax band. Any gift in a will can, however, be made to carry its own tax (which would be a pro-rata share of the total tax payable). It is therefore proper for the will to state whether any gift should be free of tax, or that the beneficiary will have to pay the relevant proportion of the tax due on the estate.

Remember also that if any of these items is not owned by the testator at the date of his death, the beneficiary will not receive that item and the clause in the will becomes void.

Clause 6 Matthew had decided that if Leslie Roberts died before him, his gift should go to his son rather than falling back into the rest of Matthew's estate. In relation to the gift to the Imperial Cancer Research Fund, the clause providing for the proper discharge of the executors if they get a receipt from an officer at the Fund means that no question that the executors had paid the money to the wrong people can later be raised by anyone entitled to part of the residuary estate. Give the full name and address as some charities have very similar names.

Clause 7 This deals with the residuary estate: all the rest of the property is left to his wife and there is the stipulation of a 30-day survivorship period. If the estate was expected to be liable for inheritance tax (IHT), the inclusion of this clause would have to be carefully considered.

Clause 8(i) This directs what happens to the property if his wife does not survive him for the appropriate period. Executors are a type of trustee. Where there is any land or houses or any leasehold interest in the estate, it is essential to have what is called a 'trust for sale' to avoid complicated legal pitfalls. The wording of clause 8(i) creates such a trust, by saying that the trustees are to sell everything and invest the proceeds, but allows them to wait as long as they like before doing so.

In a will, there is always a 'trust for sale' (even if the words are not actually used), so that the executors can administer the estate properly. They have to have sufficient cash to pay all the taxes, debts and liabilities and so the general rule is that everything must be sold to realise cash. However, so that they can keep the particular gifts given by clause 5, for example, and also keep anything that they think might be good investments, they are given a discretion to postpone the sale of anything for as long as they think fit, provided they raise sufficient cash to pay all the debts and liabilities and taxes. They are also given the power to invest or apply the money as if it were their own. This means they do not have to stick to the limited list of investments to which trustees would normally be restricted. But the executors will have to take proper advice as to the investments, not only because that is a sensible thing to do, but because the law says so.

Clause 8(ii) The children will be entitled to the property when they become 18. Matthew thought that 18 was the proper age because it is the age at which they attain their legal majority. Nevertheless, it is possible to postpone the time when the children become entitled to age 21, when they will be more mature and better able to manage their own affairs.

If you want to postpone the age at which a child will become entitled to inherit to a greater age than 21 you should take legal advice as there are a number of complications to watch.

Clause 8(iii) Matthew also thought that the age of the grandchildren should be 18 if circumstances arose in which they became entitled.

Clause 9(i) + (ii) Where infant children are entitled to property under a trust such as this, the law automatically imposes provisions (by virtue of Sections 31 and 32 of the Trustee Act 1925) that the trustees can apply any part of the income for the children's benefit, and up to one half of the capital to which they will become entitled on attaining the given age. It could be unfair on the guardians if, should the proper opportunity arise, they were to be restricted to applying only one half of the children's interest for their benefit. For instance, the children might be showing a particular aptitude for some profession or business and require more capital than one half of their prospective interest to set themselves up in that business. Such a provision is particularly relevant where children do not become entitled to the capital until the age of 21, or even older. Matthew therefore widened the provisions of the Trustee Act by saying that any part of the capital (not just up to one half) could be so used. He was quite happy to rely on the trustees' judgement. If he had not widened these powers, the trustees, who were people he particularly wanted to act as guardians for the children, might refuse to act in that capacity if they did not feel they had the freedom to do what they felt was best.

Clause 9(iii) Even if the guardians are the same people as the trustees, they have to keep separate the two different functions. If necessary, they have to give themselves receipts in their different capacities. Matthew also realised that the guardians might require a larger house but he did not want actually to give them a large sum shortly before his children became independent when his children might have more need of the money for themselves. It is important to be clear what payment will be made to the guardians from the estate so they are not out of pocket, but it is equally important not to waste capital on them, especially if the children are nearly independent when their father dies. Great care should be taken when making provision for guardians.

Applying and investing

A provision had also been included that if the trustees thought it proper they could apply (which means either transfer or sell) particular assets rather than cash '... without requiring the consent of any other person'. This phrase used to be put in as a way of saving stamp duty. That is no longer applicable, but it can sometimes result in capital gains tax savings. There is no capital gains tax payable on the death of a person, but there is if during the subsequent administration of any trust for the children, or even the period of administration of an estate, there is a sufficient capital gain between the date of death and the date of sale. Transferring assets, rather than turning them into cash to pay out, saves executors from having to sell property.

You may wish to restrict the trustees' investments to so-called 'trustee securities' which are very safe investments but tend to be of the kind that do not increase their capital value (for example, gilt-edged securities, that is, those where payment is guaranteed by the government, large building societies and public companies). But there would then be the risk that the assets will lose their capital value, and the trustees will not be able to discharge their duties properly – in which case the executors might say that they are not prepared to act. Some wills contain a clause setting out the sorts of investments that may be used. If you have complete confidence in your trustees, you can do as Matthew has done – remove all restrictions on their power to invest your property.

B. Will of a wife with young children

A wife and husband, particularly those with children, will usually each make a will in largely similar terms at the same time because they cannot know which of them is going to die first and how long there will be between their two deaths. Both of them should make provision for what is to happen if the other one dies first; the wills should, therefore, be in largely the same form.

Emma's will takes the same form as Matthew's; they agreed, in particular, about the appointment of the guardians. For clause 2, however, Emma wished her cousin Edward Seymour Forbes to be the other executor instead of her brother-in-law David Gordon Seaton, but she also specified that if her cousin died before her then her brother-in-law David Gordon Seaton should be the executor instead.

Emma directed in clause 4 that she wished her body to be buried; she had no particular wishes in relation to donating organs for transplant.

In clauses 5 and 6 she bequeathed her diamond earrings to her niece Luisa Forbes and, apart from £250 to her potential executors, left legacies of £50 each to Sally and Martina Saunders who had been her bridesmaids.

Except for substituting 'my husband Matthew John Seaton' where appropriate, the important clauses 7, 8 and 9 in her will were the same as in his.

In both Matthew's and Emma's wills they included a 30-day survivorship period as Matthew's estate was below the IHT threshold. If the estate of either were larger it would be wise to consider giving some of it to the other so that both could give larger legacies to the children, thus taking advantage of the £215,000 nil-rate band available on each death.

Matthew and Emma have provided for a number of situations which may or may not arise over the coming few years. They can revoke or alter the will at any time before their death. Although Matthew should be aware of the tax consequences of his will, he should not allow the desire for tax avoidance to prevent a proper provision for Emma, and *vice versa*.

C. Will of an elderly single person

An elderly person who is single, divorced or widowed (and probably has few relatives) might wish to leave all his property without any complications to one or two people. Because of his age, these are often people who are also elderly. To avoid the risk of an intestacy, there should be provision for what should happen to the property if the nominated beneficiaries die before the testator.

Take, for example, the very simple will of John Ryder who is 75 years old. He is a widower and his only living relative is his son, David Ryder, who is unmarried and 40 years old.

His will could read like this:

WILL of John Ryder of 142 Chiltern Court, Thoden Gardens, Hastings, Sussex.
1. I revoke all previous wills and codicils.
2. I appoint my son David Ryder of 15 West Wind Way, Hastings, Sussex, to be the sole executor of my will and I leave to him all my property of whatever description.
3. In the event that my son David Ryder shall die before me I appoint X of ..... and Y of ..... to be my executors and trustees and I give all my property to the World Wide Fund for Nature (address) and the Musicians' Benevolent Fund (address) in equal shares and I declare that the receipt of the persons professing to be the proper officers of those institutions shall be a full and sufficient discharge for my trustees.

Date:

Signature:

Signed by John Ryder in our presence and then by us in his:

Witness 1: [signature, address, occupation]

Witness 2: [signature, address, occupation]

Clause 3 would apply only after the death of the person whom he had appointed as sole executor. Someone else would therefore need to administer the estate – hence the need for trustees. If David Ryder dies before his father, the two charities will benefit in equal shares from the whole estate. It is very important to put in executors who can arrange your funeral and secure your house at short notice, especially if you have no spouse.

Such a will can also be the pattern for that of a husband and wife who have no children or other relatives; the beneficiary and executor would usually therefore be the other spouse.

D. Will of a divorced/separated person

If the testator wishes to avoid any benefit going to the previous or separated spouse, legal advice should be sought because there can be complications: the former spouse might make an application to the court for a share in the estate regardless of the terms of the will, particularly if the division of the matrimonial property has not been finalised or if the testator was still paying maintenance at the time of his death. Show your adviser any order of the divorce court dealing with matrimonial assets or maintenance.

If the testator has a new partner whom he wishes to benefit for the rest of her life but thereafter he wishes his property to go back to his own family, or children by his previous marriage perhaps, legal advice should be sought because it involves the complicated trust provision of giving a life interest to a person, with the property then reverting after the death of that person and not passing in accordance with the original beneficiary's will or the rules governing the distribution of that person's estate on an intestacy. In these circumstances, it would be better for you not to attempt to draft your own will. Remember that legal aid (green form advice) may be available in some cases – ask at your local Citizens Advice Bureau for the names of solicitors who provide this.

E. Will of a husband/wife with grown-up children

Where there are adult children and the total family assets exceed £215,000, a will requires some consideration from the inheritance tax point of view. If you are certain that your spouse does not need the whole of your estate to maintain him/her for the rest of his/her life, you should consider giving some of your property direct to your children to avoid the aggregation of your own estate with your spouse's on the death of the survivor.

If you have made substantial gifts within the last seven years, you could, however, consider leaving your spouse a specific sum of money or property, which will not be taxed, even if that would dispose of most of your estate, and give the residuary estate (out of which IHT will be paid) to your children.

The will should take a similar form to the others considered above, but the clauses dealing with the distribution of the property might run something like this:

> To my wife Marion I give all my interest in the property known as 5 High Street, Hughtown, or such other freehold or leasehold property as shall be our main residence at the time of my death and the sum of £150,000 absolutely.
>
> I give the whole of the rest of my estate to my executors as trustees. They are to sell everything not in the form of cash but they may postpone the sale of anything for as long as they like. After paying my debts any taxes and duties payable on my death and the expenses of my funeral and of administering my estate they are to hold what is left upon trust to pay and transfer the same to such of my children John Frank and Diana as survive me and if more than one then in equal shares absolutely.

If your estate is worth more than £215,000 you may hit a problem if you make a large tax-free bequest to, say, a daughter and then give what is left to your spouse (who is exempt from IHT). The law states that the value of the tax-free gift must then be 'grossed up' to include the tax payable as well as the gift. Seek advice if this looks likely.

If there have been no gifts during the last seven years and provided you are happy that your spouse would have sufficient to maintain her (him) for the rest of her life, then substantial savings of inheritance tax can still be made by giving legacies only to the extent of the nil-rate band for inheritance tax, leaving all the residue to your spouse. Your spouse would do the same, although it might be necessary to equalise your estate in order to make the most of this action. The legacies to be given, which could therefore total up to £215,000, need not necessarily be to your children but could be to any taxable beneficiary.

The clauses dealing with the distribution of the property could be as follows:

I give the following legacies free from all taxes and duties payable on or by reference to my death
  (i) To my daughter Barbara the sum of £40,000
  (ii) To my daughter Francesca the sum of £40,000
  (iii) To my son Matthew the sum of £40,000
  (iv) To my friend Jeremy Mitchell the sum of £40,000
  (v) To my friend John Bull the sum of £19,000
I give the following bequests free from all taxes and duties payable on or by reference to my death:
  (i) To my friend Edward Raleigh of Kingswood, Lymington Drive, Poole, Dorset, my stamp collection
  (ii) To my brother Andrew Basil my car
  (iii) To my son Matthew my collection of prints
  (v) To my daughter Francesca my clocks watches and cut glassware
I give the rest of my estate to my wife Marjorie if she survives me. If my wife Marjorie dies before me then I leave my remaining personal effects furniture and chattels to my daughter Francesca and the rest of my estate shall be divided equally between my three children Barbara Francesca and Matthew absolutely.

On the basis that the bequests of individual items amount to approximately £5,000, the total sum of the legacies and bequests of £184,000 used up most of the nil-rate band.

F. Will of an unmarried couple with no children

As mentioned on page 69, a will is usually revoked on marriage. If an unmarried couple are contemplating marriage and wish to avoid this problem, they should insert a clause at the beginning of their respective wills; it could read as follows:

  1. This will shall not be revoked by my intended marriage to [Partner's name].

If no time limit is inserted, the will remains valid even if the relationship breaks up.

If the couple want their wills to take effect only on their wedding then the clause could read:

  1. This will is made in contemplation of and is conditional upon my marriage to [Partner's name].

In the latter case, however, it should be borne in mind that until the wedding the parties will be intestate. It is therefore much better to use the first alternative unless there is some special reason for the latter.

If, on the other hand, an unmarried couple have no intention of getting married, then they should simply make their wills in the usual way without either of the above clauses. They should not forget that the surviving spouse exemption (see page 18) does not apply to cohabiting couples and that other benefits such as widow's pension will not be available.

Unmarried couples may want their own property to revert to their own family rather than to go to the family of the survivor, or perhaps to the family of someone else whom the survivor may marry or live with in the future and who would then benefit through the survivor's own will.

There are a number of ways of dealing with this. Bear in mind that it cannot be known in advance which partner will die first, nor the period of time between the two deaths. It may be five minutes, five days, or fifty years. Some couples feel that provided it is obvious that the survivor will have a long life after the death of the first person to die, then it is right and proper for the survivor to benefit absolutely from all of the property. To make sure, the survivorship period may be extended to three or even six months, in the case of some common accident, so that the property will pass in accordance with the will of the first to die.

The only other way in which the first partner to die can be certain that his property will revert to his own family on the death of the survivor is to limit the benefit of the survivor to a 'life interest only', allowing the survivor the use of the property for her life and then dictating who benefits from that property on the death of the survivor e.g. his own family. This, however, involves complicated trust provisions and a solicitor should be consulted.

A couple's most valuable asset is usually their house or flat, owned either as joint tenants or as tenants-in-common. Careful consideration should be given in deciding what provisions to include in your will as far as the house or flat is concerned because if it is owned as tenants-in-common then the will of the first to die will operate on that person's specified beneficial share in the ownership of the property. If the property is owned as joint tenants then the whole property automatically passes to the survivor irrespective of anything the will may say.

Sometimes the mortgage on any property would be paid off on the death of the first partner by the proceeds of an endowment or mortgage protection insurance policy.

Unmarried couples with children either of their own or by virtue of any previous association should seek legal advice as to the terms of their wills.

Once the form and words of the will have been finally decided and the will has been typed, it must be signed. There are strict rules for dealing with this.

Signing the will (execution)

A will does not have to state the date on which it was signed, but there will be problems obtaining probate if it does not; the date can appear at the beginning or the end. Perhaps if it is at the end, just above the place for signing, there is less chance of forgetting to fill in the date when the will is actually signed. There is no need to set out the date in full – 'the twenty-seventh day of November one thousand nine hundred and ninety-seven' – or to say 'in the year of Our Lord ...' There is nothing wrong with putting '27 November 1997', provided it is written legibly in the space on the will meant for it. The date should be put in before the will is finally signed in the presence of the witnesses.

Witnesses to the signature

No one who is left anything in the will should be a witness, and neither should the wife or husband of anyone who is left anything in it. Where this happens, the will is legally valid – in other words, these witnesses are perfectly all right as witnesses – but they lose their legacies; the will is interpreted as if the gift to the witness, or the spouse of the witness, were cut out of it. Similarly, a person appointed as executor should not be a witness. If he is, the will is valid, and so is the appointment, but any legacy to the executor would not be and he would not even be able to reclaim his costs from the estate or, if he is a professional person, would not be able to charge for administering the estate because any charging clause in the will would be invalidated.

A blind person should not be a witness. Also, it is probably more sensible to avoid having someone under the age of 18 to be a witness, although there is nothing in law to prevent it.

The will must be signed by the testator, the person whose will it is, within the sight of two witnesses, who should both be present together when he actually signs.

It will be invalid unless both the witnesses are physically present when the will is signed. Strictly speaking, it is still a valid will if the testator acknowledges his previously written signature – as distinct from signing there and then – in the joint presence of the two witnesses. It is best that they should both actually watch as the signature goes on, although it is sufficient if they are standing or sitting in a position with a direct line of sight so that they could have seen the signing if they had looked in the right direction.

The testator must sign first, and the witnesses afterwards; the other way around will not do.

Each witness must sign in the presence of the testator, but one witness does not have to be present when the other witness is signing. If Matthew Seaton were to sign his will in the presence of Robert Jones and Michael Smith, and then, before either of them began to sign, Matthew went out of the room, and while he was out of the room, Robert and Michael signed as witnesses, the will would be invalid. The same would apply if only one of the witnesses signed out of the presence of the testator, but it would be valid if Matthew remained after signing in the presence of both the witnesses, and Robert left the room while Michael signed and then Matthew was still present when Robert returned.

To sum up, then:

- the person making the will must be there all the time that anybody is signing
- both the witnesses must be there when the testator signs
- it is not necessary for each witness to be present when the other witness signs.

To be on the safe side, however, the best thing is to make sure that all three of them are present throughout all the signing by all three of them.

Attestation clause

The will should contain an attestation clause, that is, a clause explaining the process of signing and witnessing. If the clause were missing, then, after the testator's death, when it comes to proving the will, it would be necessary to have an affidavit – a sworn statement – from one of the witnesses to explain what happened when the will was signed and witnessed. This could cause great difficulties if the witnesses could not be traced, or were dead. So a properly worded attestation clause, though not strictly necessary, should be included in a will.

The Principal Probate Registry and the District Registries will accept the following attestation clause: 'Signed by the testator (testatrix) in our presence and then by us in his (hers).'

It is also not strictly necessary for the witnesses to write their addresses on the will. Their signature is all that is legally required. But, once again, it is much better if they do add their address, and perhaps their occupation as well, so that if there were any question raised later about what happened at the time, they can more easily be traced. For the same reason, it is a good idea to write the name in block letters underneath the signature.

When the will is long

If your will runs to more than one page, sign each page at the bottom, and ask the witnesses to do the same, immediately after the last line of writing, without leaving any gap. This is not a legal requirement, but it does help to prevent any forgery of your will, in the form of adding a clause to the bottom of a page, or even an extra page. If, after your death, a clause saying 'I give £5,000 to William Sykes' appeared at the foot of a page, you would not be there to explain that it was not there when you signed the will.

Signing each page is more important still when the will extends to more than one sheet of paper. It is better not to leave blank the back page of any sheet of paper on which your will is written. Either continue with the clauses on to the back of each page, or draw a line right across the blank space, and put your initials at the top and bottom of the line. Ask the witnesses to do the same. The aim should be to make any tampering with your will as difficult as possible, and to make it obvious which are the sheets of paper which comprise your will, each sheet of which should bear your signature at the bottom. Make sure that each page of your will is numbered, so that no one can craftily slip in a couple of extra pages containing benefits to himself. Finally, do not pin or clip anything to your will and make sure that no pin holes appear in it. Such holes, or marks where a paper clip has been attached, may give the impression that a sheet of paper forming part of your will was at one time attached to it, but has now disappeared.

In Matthew's will, therefore, he and the two witnesses, as well as signing the full attestation at the end of the will, should each sign at the bottom of the first page. If below the witnesses' signatures on the back of the sheet there is more than the usual bottom-of-a-page space, it is also sensible to 'line-off' the space, and for Matthew and the witnesses to sign each end of the line.

Picking up Matthew Seaton's will at the last part of the last clause as it was prepared, when the process of signing and witnessing is over, it will continue through to the end to look like this:

... shall be a full and sufficient discharge to my trustees in respect of that beneficiary.
Date: 27 November 1997
Signature: M. J. Seaton
Signed by Matthew John Seaton in our presence and then by us in his:

Margery Abrahams	M. Roberts
MARGERY ABRAHAMS	MICHAEL ROBERTS
22 Twintree Avenue	'The Reddings', Park Avenue
Minford, Surrey	Little Minford, Surrey
Sales Manager	Schoolmaster

M. A.   M.R.

What to do with the will

From the moment the will is signed and witnessed it is valid. Matthew Seaton can die at any time secure in the knowledge that his testamentary wishes have been legally expressed.

There is no law in England and Wales requiring that wills must be registered before death. It is up to the testator himself to find a safe place for his will, to put it there, and to let his executors know where it is. Tell them when the will has been made, where it is, and confirm that the will appoints them as executors.

Quite a few people lodge their will in their bank, but this often leads to problems or delay with its release following death. If you have a safe at home, this is an obvious place in which to put your will. Failing that, perhaps the best place for your will is wherever you keep your other important documents: marriage and birth certificates, savings certificates, title deeds of the house, and so on. Put the will in an envelope and seal it, and write on the outside your full name, the word WILL in large letters and the date. There is no stamp duty on a will, so no further formalities are required before putting the will away safely.

If the will is lodged at the bank, it may be helpful to make the executor known to the bank, perhaps even introduce him or her personally to the manager, so that there will be no difficulty or delay about handing over the will to the executor. If the will is locked away in your house or your office, tell the executor where the key is.

Whether or not you tell your executors (or your relatives) who is going to inherit your property under your will is entirely up to you; there is no legal requirement. But you should keep your executors informed about what you possess. A list, setting out in round figures what you own, could well be placed with your will for safe custody, and from time to time you should revise the list to keep it up to date.

You should, perhaps, have told your executors, when asking whether they were willing to accept the appointment, what your property consisted of, its approximate value and what you want to happen to it after your death, and if you have appointed guardians for any children, so that they knew in advance the measure of the job they were being asked to take on. As time goes by, and your situation develops and changes, they should be kept informed on how your current wealth stands, especially if you acquire unusual assets. Your object should be to make things as easy as possible for them when you die. Any tendency to be secretive about your assets is likely to make life more difficult for your executors.

You should also keep them up to date on where the essential documents are to be found. The logical course, obviously, is to keep things like share certificates, building society account books, savings certificates, insurance policies, title deeds and all similar documents in one place – a family safe, for instance, or a locked drawer. This may be the same place where you keep your will. If you keep your affairs tidy and orderly so far as possible, when the time comes for your executors to act, they will not find that they have taken on an investigation, instead of an administration. Age Concern England* has published a useful four-page form, *Instructions for my next-of-kin and executors*, on which to fill in a host of details, including a 'where to find things' list (including the will), and personal/financial information that will be useful to executors when the time comes for them to act.

Depositing a will

If you want to, you can deposit your will at Somerset House. If you write to the Record Keeper at the Principal Registry of the Family Division,* you will be sent a large envelope and instructions about completing all the details requested on it, signing and witnessing, and where it should be taken or sent. A small fee is payable. You will be given a deposit certificate which has to be produced if the will is to be withdrawn. The Administration of Justice Act 1982 will eventually establish a new system for the deposit and registration of wills.

There is no special advantage in depositing a will in this formal manner (rather than, say, putting it in a safe or depositing it with your bank). It does not prevent future wills or codicils being made.

Alterations

Bear in mind that you can change your will at any time. You may want to alter your will because of a change in circumstances, such as a birth or a death, or a change of heart following a difference of opinion, for instance. You may also want to change your will for tax reasons, perhaps because you have just made a very large gift (and there is, of course, no guarantee that you will live another seven years), or change your will because seven years have now elapsed since you made any large gifts or because there have been changes in tax law.

You must not cross bits out of your will, or write bits in, or make any alterations whatsoever on it. The will is valid in the form in which it stood on the day it was signed. Any obvious alterations made on the face of a will are presumed – until the contrary is proved – to have been made after the original signing and witnessing took place, and so not to form part of the legally valid will. Furthermore, any legacy which appears underneath your signature is not valid.

Theoretically, you could make subsequent alterations on the will itself by signing the altered will and having that new signature witnessed again, as was done when the will was first signed. But this is messy and unsatisfactory, and quite the wrong way to go about making alterations to a will.

Codicils

If all you want to do is to make a simple alteration to your will as it stands, either by revoking any provision or by adding something, you could do this by making a codicil. This really is nothing more than a supplement to a will, which makes some alteration to it but leaves the rest of it standing. For instance, you may wish to increase a cash legacy to take account of inflation since you made the will, or reallocate a bequest because the intended recipient has died.

A codicil can also be useful for changing the executors or guardians in a will. The guardians you have chosen may become separated or divorced, or they may now have a handicapped child so that it would be an unfair burden on them to be responsible for your children, too. A codicil can include a provision revoking the appointment and substituting others. A codicil can also be used to specify that a will previously made should be 'in anticipation of marriage', using the clause contained in Will F on page 58. In this way the subsequent marriage will not revoke the will.

A codicil, to be valid, must be signed and witnessed in exactly the same way as a will. It has to be signed by the testator in the presence of two witnesses and they must both sign it in the presence of the testator. These witnesses do not have to be the same two who witnessed the original will. Here is an example:

This is the first codicil to the will dated 27 November 1997 of me Matthew John Seaton of 14 Twintree Avenue, Minford, Surrey.
1. I revoke the bequest of my golf clubs bag and trolley to my nephew Donald Millington.
2. I give £250 to my brother Robert Seaton.
3. In all other respects I confirm my will.

Date: 20 December 1997
Signature: M. J. Seaton

Signed by Matthew John Seaton in our presence and then by us in his:

Ivy Gurney	*P. G. Ambrose*
IVY GURNEY	PETER GRAEME AMBROSE
'The Larches'	36a Wolf Street
Greta Grove	Hallford, Surrey
Eastbourne, Sussex	Concert artist
Bookseller	

Provided it contains a clause in the terms of clause 3 then a codicil acts as a confirmation of everything contained in the will that has not been expressly revoked by the codicil, and the will has to be construed as at the date of the codicil. To find out the whole of the testator's wishes, both the will and the codicil have to be considered.

There is no limit on how many codicils you may make. Some people make quite a few. But a codicil is suitable only for a straightforward alteration to a will. For anything more than that, it is better to make a completely new will. If the will was quite short in the first place, it is probably better to make a completely new will anyway, and not bother with making a codicil.

Revocation

If you make a later will, it should contain the clause which revokes the previous will. Once the later will is signed, and so in force, it is best to destroy the previous one, just in case, years later when you die, the old will is found among your papers and mistaken for the one you meant to apply. Or at least be sure to mark clearly on the previous one 'Revoked by will/codicil dated ...' so that if it is found among your papers it cannot be mistaken for your latest will or codicil. If you do not destroy the older document, then if for any reason the later document were held to be invalid, the older will would still be operative. Otherwise you could die intestate, which might also not be in the interest of people to whom you wish to leave your property.

By destruction

There are two other ways of revoking a will apart from a specific clause in a later will mentioning revocation. The first is where, with the intention of revoking it, you burn it, tear it up, or in some other way destroy it. The emphasis here is on the words 'with the intention of revoking it'. If your will were to be accidentally burnt, whether by you or by someone else, it would not be revoked by that. There have, in fact, been cases where a will has been declared valid after the testator's death, the original having been accidentally destroyed. In one case, for instance, the torn-up pieces were reassembled and proved as a valid will, where it was shown that it was torn up in mistake for an old letter.

The testator himself must burn the will, or tear it up, in order for it to be effectively revoked. Alternatively, it may be done by someone at his direction and in his presence. But your will would not be revoked, for example, if you were to write to the bank manager who kept it, telling him to destroy it, even if he did so. The destruction has to take place in your presence – otherwise it does not revoke the will.

By marriage

The other way of revoking a will is surprising and is one not always remembered: getting married. The law supposes that a man or a woman who has made a will and later gets married automatically wishes that the will should no longer stand. As a result, merely to get married, without saying anything about an existing will, revokes the will. The whole will is revoked, including any legacies to people wholly independent of the new husband or wife.

This can have some curious results. Imagine that a widow with young children has made a will leaving her property to the children. Some years later she marries again. She must make a new will just before the marriage and with a clause stating that it is in the anticipation of the marriage to the second husband; otherwise, her husband would inherit all the property up to £125,000, her children possibly getting nothing, as she would have died intestate, her will having been revoked by her second marriage. If she waits until after the marriage it is possible she could die just after the marriage before she has had a chance to make the new will.

Not always revoked by marriage

It is, however, possible to make a will which says that it is made in contemplation of a forthcoming marriage.

The will must state that it is made in contemplation of marriage to a particular person, who must be named, and it must also state that the testator intends that the will shall not be revoked by his marriage to that person. Such a will is not revoked by that marriage but, should that marriage never happen and, instead, the testator marries someone else, the will is then revoked. If no marriage whatever takes place, the will, of course, will remain effective, unless it was made conditional on the particular contemplated marriage taking place within a certain period of time. It is essential to have legal advice on these matters, although some of the provisions necessary are found in Will F on page 58.

The effect of divorce

Divorce, on the other hand, does not automatically revoke all the provisions of a will. The effect of a divorce is that any appointment of the former spouse as an executor will be of no effect, and any gift in the will to the former spouse will be treated as if the former spouse had died before the testator. Where the gift is a specific one, for example of a house or '£10,000', such property will go to whomever is entitled to the residue of the estate. But where, under the terms of the will, the former spouse is given the residue of the estate, it will be dealt with in accordance with the intestacy rules.

If Matthew and Emma (of the earlier examples of Wills A and B) had divorced and no alterations were made to the wills, then the executors of Will A would have been David Seaton and Andrew Shervington. Clause 7 would have been of no effect and until a few years ago it would have been possible to say categorically that clause 8 would have taken effect as if Emma had died before Matthew, and the rest of the will, including the legacies in clauses 5 and 6, would remain unaffected. However, a decided case has now determined that in these circumstances, although Emma will lose her benefit from Matthew's estate, the rest of the property will pass in accordance with the intestacy rules rather than the subsequent provision of the will, such as clause 8 in Matthew's will.

If you are contemplating divorce, it is possible to cover this situation by executing a short codicil before the decree is pronounced, amending the circumstances in which the children will benefit to include the divorce. This would read along these lines: '... in clause 8 of my will after "does not survive me for the period of thirty days" shall be inserted the words "or we are divorced at the time of my death" ...'. But it is best to make a new will on divorce.

Later

Once you have made a will, it is easy to tuck it away safely and forget about it for ever. But you should review your will now and again: every couple of years is not too frequent. You may find that nothing needs changing. On the other hand, there could be quite substantial changes that need to be made. If so, you will have to start the whole process over again.

CHAPTER 4

IN SCOTLAND

ALL matters of tax, IHT and its exemptions, the 'seven-year rule' regarding lifetime gifts and gifts with reservation apply in Scotland. Apart from that, there are some considerable differences in law, practice and procedure. The following pages give an indication of some of the main differences between Scottish law and what has been said about the law as it applies in England and Wales.

Intestacy

The rules of intestacy for persons dying domiciled in Scotland (that is, when Scotland is regarded as their permanent home) are very different. The widow(er) gets the house (up to £110,000 in value), furniture excluding the car (up to £20,000 in value), and a cash sum of £30,000 if the deceased leaves children or other descendants, but £50,000 if there are no surviving children or other descendants. He or she also gets a proportion of the remainder of the moveable estate. Moveable estate means roughly everything except land and buildings. The children inherit everything else.

If there is no widow(er), the children inherit the whole estate.

Where the deceased leaves neither a widow(er) nor children or other descendants, the estate is divided equally between his or her parents and brothers and sisters (or their descendants). Failing these, uncles and aunts (or their descendants) inherit, then grandparents, then great-uncles and great-aunts (or their descendants), then great-grandparents and so on until someone is found to inherit.

This is only a brief description. A fuller explanation of the Scottish intestacy rules is on pages 206–11.

Who can make a will

In Scotland, children aged twelve or over can make valid wills if their permanent home is in Scotland.

Legal rights

In Scotland, you cannot disinherit your husband or wife or descendants completely. Your husband or wife has a right to one-third of your moveable estate whatever the will says. This fraction is increased to one half if you do not leave any descendants. Similarly, the children between them have a right to one third, or one half if you do not leave a widow(er).

These rights are called 'legal rights'. A person claiming legal rights simply has to inform the executors. It is necessary to go to court only if the executors refuse to pay and the legal rights have to be enforced. Your husband, wife or children must choose between their legal rights and what (if anything) they have been left by your will. They cannot have both.

But legal rights are due from moveable estate only. If most of the value of your estate is in land or buildings, your moveable estate will be relatively small and legal rights will be worth little.

It is possible to disinherit your children by dying without a will. Provided your estate is not too valuable, your widow(er)'s rights to the house, furniture and cash will swallow up the whole estate, leaving nothing for the children. On the other hand, if you had left a will leaving everything to your husband or wife, your children could have claimed their legal rights to one-third of your moveable estate.

Death of beneficiary

A person has to survive the deceased by only an instant in order to inherit. Where it cannot be ascertained who died first the younger is deemed to have survived the elder, except in the case of a husband and wife where neither is deemed to have survived the other.

If the person to whom you leave the legacy dies before you the legacy lapses. Generally, the lapsed legacy either becomes part of the residue (if the legacy was of specified property) or intestate estate (if the legacy was the residue or a share of residue). But this general rule does not apply to a legacy to your child, nephew or niece or one of their descendants who was alive when you made the will but who died before you, leaving issue who survive you. In this case the issue will take the lapsed legacy, unless *your will makes it very clear that this is not to happen. Merely providing for an alternative beneficiary is not enough to prevent the issue from taking the legacy.*

Wills and executors

The Public Trustee service is not available in Scotland.

All executors who are nominated in the will and who survive the deceased are entitled to act. Unless an executor declines to act, he or she will be confirmed.

In all but the simplest estate, it is probably better to have two executors, to guard against a sole executor dying before completing the administration.

A will which sets up a trust should empower the trustees to sell any items. This avoids doubt about their statutory power to sell, for example, the family home or items which are not investments.

Scottish trustees have only limited power to use income and none to advance capital from the estate for the children's benefit or to buy a house other than as a residence for the children unless there are express clauses in the will or the court sanctions these steps. You should get a solicitor to prepare your will if you want to set up a trust.

Co-ownership of property

Property owned by two people in Scotland is owned in common. Each owner has a share which on death passes under his or her will or under the intestacy rules.

The equivalent of a joint tenancy (in England) is (in Scotland) common ownership with a survivorship destination in the title to the property, the destination transferring the share of the first to die to the survivor.

You cannot change a survivorship destination except by rearranging the title. This requires the consent of your co-owner and the deeds should be prepared by a solicitor. A survivorship destination usually prevents you leaving your share of the property by will to anybody other than your co-owner. If you are able to leave your share as you like (for example, where you paid for the whole property entirely out of your own money), you must revoke the destination by referring to it in your will and specifically cancelling it. Failure to do this will mean that your share will pass to your co-owner because an unrevoked destination prevails over a will.

Signing the will

A will in Scotland is valid if it is signed and witnessed or simply signed.

Witnessed wills

In the case of a witnessed will one witness is sufficient. The witness must see the testator sign the will or the testator must acknowledge his or her signature to the witness. Where the will is on more than one sheet of paper, each page (except the last) is signed at the foot by the testator, and the last page is signed at the end by the testator and the witness. The name and address of the witness must be given either at the end of the will in what is called the testing clause (see example below) or below his or her signature. The testing clause also contains the date of signing the will. A typical example would run as follows:

> IN WITNESS WHEREOF I have signed this will [on this and the preceding two pages] at Edinburgh on 9 December 1996 before the witness James Mowat, Bank Accountant, of 54 Marchmont Gardens, Edinburgh.
>
> [James Mowat, witness]   [Testator's signature]

The witness need not know what the document is about. Any person aged 16 or over can be a witness. Witnesses do not lose their legacies but you should avoid having your will witnessed by beneficiaries as that makes the will easier to challenge.

Blind people may sign their own wills, but they and people who cannot write may use another method. This involves a solicitor, advocate, sheriff clerk or justice of the peace reading the will to the testator and signing it after receiving the testator's authority to do so. The signature should be witnessed as above.

Wills made before 1 August 1995 had to have two witnesses.

Signed will

A will is valid if it is simply signed by the testator at the end. However, if challenged it has to be proved to be genuine. A witnessed will on the other hand is presumed to be genuine unless the challengers can prove it is false. A will that is merely signed will not be accepted for confirmation (see page 192) unless a court is satisfied that it is genuine. The procedure is fairly simple and requires two people each to produce a sworn statement (called an affidavit) that the will is genuine and the signature is that of the testator. The cost will be about £150, but if there is any dispute the court will require to hear evidence from witnesses and perhaps handwriting experts and the cost will be very much greater.

Wills made before 1 August 1995 were valid if simply signed by the testator only if the will was entirely in the testator's own handwriting (a holograph will) or if the testator had written by hand above his or her signature at the end of the typed will the words 'adopted as holograph'.

Afterwards

There are no facilities for depositing your will in an official depository in Scotland while you are alive. Although you could record your will in the Books of Council and Session – a national register of deeds kept at Edinburgh and open to public inspection – recording wills of living people in practice is never done because it is impossible to retrieve them or cancel their recording.

After confirmation, a Scottish will can be inspected at the sheriff court which granted the confirmation. Some, but not all, wills are also registered in the Books of Council and Session after death but before confirmation.

Revocation of a will

Your will is revoked if it is destroyed on your instructions even though you are not present to see it done.

In Scotland, a person's will is not automatically revoked by his or her subsequent marriage. When you get married, you should consider making a new will with gifts to your husband or wife. Unless you do, your husband or wife will not benefit under your will, although he or she can claim 'legal rights'.

You may also want to include your new stepchildren in your will. They have to be specifically included in your will – otherwise they will get nothing. This is because a legacy to 'my children' will not benefit your stepchildren, nor can they claim 'legal rights' out of your estate.

Bequests to your husband or wife are not automatically invalidated by your subsequent divorce. Whether your ex-husband or ex-wife would still benefit under your will depends on the exact wording of the will. So it is better to put the matter beyond doubt by making a new will whether you wish him or her to continue to benefit or to get nothing.

Scottish law presumes that if a child is born to you after making a will you would wish to make a new will including the addition to your family. Your existing will may do this by a gift to be shared 'among all my children'. But where there is no provision for children or where the children to benefit are named and the will fails to make provision for a later child, he or she can apply to the court for it to be set aside. Only the child can apply to the court, however much others may wish your will to be set aside. The court will set it aside unless it is satisfied that you intended to exclude the child rather than simply never got round to altering your will. If your will is set aside, your estate will be divided according to the intestacy rules. This may be of no help to the child; he or she may be better off letting your will stand and claiming 'legal rights'.

CHAPTER 5

Probate

This part of the book explains how to administer the estate of someone who has died. The table on pages 84–5 shows the essential steps which have to be taken and some of the decisions to be made. If any complicated situations arise, you may have to consult a solicitor. Usually, however, you should be able to cope quite easily with the matters which can arise when dealing with a straightforward estate.

Personal representatives

The people who deal with what you own when you die are called your personal representatives. If they are appointed by a valid will or codicil, they are known as executors; when they are not appointed in this way, as happens on an intestacy, the personal representatives are known as administrators.

In either case, they will usually have to obtain an official document from the High Court to show that they are the ones with legal authority to deal with the property. In the case of executors, who are said to 'prove' the will, this document is called a grant of probate, also referred to as a probate of the will, or, for short, the probate. Administrators, on the other hand, obtain a grant of letters of administration. The document which constitutes the probate or the letters of administration is sometimes referred to as the grant. The task of executors as well as of administrators is referred to as the administration of the estate.

A valid will operates from the moment its maker dies, so that an executor has full authority from the moment of a person's death. That authority is effective, even though the will has not yet been formally proved in the way the law demands. When eventually the will is proved, by the issue to the executors of a grant of probate, it merely confirms and makes official the powers they have had since the testator's death.

An important distinction between probate and letters of administration is that administrators have no legal authority to act until the grant of letters of administration is issued to them.

It can happen that there is a fully valid will which does not appoint executors or where the executors cannot act (because they have died) or have renounced. In this case, the nearest relatives will usually apply for letters of administration. This can cause difficulty if the family does not get on. It makes it hard to decide who will arrange the funeral and who will take charge of the house. The procedures for making the application are the same as for executors, but whereas executors at the end of an administration receive a grant of probate, in this case it will be a grant of letters of administration with the will annexed, that is, the terms of the will will be attached to the letters of administration. Even though they are administrators and not executors, they have to deal with the distribution of the estate in accordance with the will – the rules of intestacy will not apply.

When no grant is needed

It is not always necessary to take out a grant of probate or letters of administration. If the property left behind consists only of cash (that is, bank notes and coins) and personal effects such as furniture and a car (and not, for instance, any shares, bank accounts, pension arrears or house), no formal steps to prove the right of the relatives to their inheritance need be taken. But the will should never be destroyed in case of a dispute later.

There are some other kinds of property which can be handed over without much formality. Where, for instance, the deceased held not more than £5,000 in any one form of National Savings (including any interest due or prizes on premium bonds), that amount (together with the interest to the date of payment) can be paid to the person now entitled to it, without a grant being taken out at all. The same applies to money held in certain pension funds and friendly societies. The total of sums in the savings bank (or similar) must not exceed £5,000, but the total value of the estate (including the money in the savings bank) may be more than £5,000. The procedure for obtaining the money is usually simple. The relative or other person who is entitled to claim the money writes to the savings bank or other organisation concerned, explaining the circumstances, and asking to be sent the appropriate form (for National Savings, form DNS 904 is also available at post offices). This must then be completed – see page 95 – and returned with a death certificate ('certificate for certain statutory purposes', obtained from the registrar of deaths) and, where appropriate, the marriage certificate (or a photocopy of it). (However, the National Savings department or other body can, at its discretion, require you to take out a grant even if the amount involved is under £5,000.)

Nomination

There was a system of nominating some kinds of property in favour of a particular person, to take effect on death, for example the money in a National Savings Bank account, and National Savings certificates and certain specified government stock. Since 1981, no new nominations can be made but such nominations as are in existence will be honoured.

The person to whom savings were nominated can apply to have them in cash or transferred into his or her name, on producing the death certificate and without producing a grant of probate or letters of administration.

Nomination is quite distinct from the procedure for obtaining payment in cases under £5,000, and applies irrespective of the amount involved. But if the savings bank has any doubts as to the size of the estate involved, it may require a certificate from the Inland Revenue to show that the inheritance tax (IHT) has been taken care of. (Nomination is not a way of escaping IHT: the amount that has been nominated has to be accounted for as part of the estate.)

A nomination that was made in this way applies whether or not a will mentions it and is not revoked or affected by a will made afterwards. A nomination is revoked by signing the special form, or by the death of the person in whose favour the nomination was made before the death of the person who made it (and also by the marriage of the nominator).

Joint property

Also, no probate would be required if all the property in the estate (houses, bank accounts, etc.) is in joint names as joint tenants, one of whom survives. In this case, the property automatically becomes wholly owned by the surviving joint owner and all that is required is to register the death certificate with the appropriate authority such as company registrar, Land Registry or bank (but inheritance tax may be payable on the half value of the assets).

Accounting to the Inland Revenue

Even where probate is not required, the Inland Revenue rules demand an account of all property in the estate, if the value of the estate – including the total value of all jointly held property, together with all taxable gifts in the past ten years – is more than £180,000. An Inland Revenue account has to be completed by the executors even if they do not need to ask for a grant of probate.

Whether or not a grant of probate is needed does not depend on the size of the estate, but on the type of assets. It is necessary where some documents need to be signed before an asset can be transferred or a sale can be effected. A grant of probate would be needed even if only one life policy were involved, or some other asset worth, say, £15,000 and no inheritance tax were payable.

What is involved in administration

In most cases, personal representatives will have to deal with the following matters:

- find out if there is a will or not, and who will be the executor or administrator

- find out the nature and value of the assets in the estate
- find out details of the debts (advertise for creditors, if relevant – see page 149)
- prepare a detailed list of the estate and of the debts, for the purpose of IHT
- work out the amount of IHT payable and arrange any necessary overdraft or other credit. If there is sufficient money in a building society account, arrangements can be made to use that money
- prepare and send off the documents required by the Inland Revenue and Probate Registry
- pay the IHT
- visit the Probate Registry in person to swear the papers
- receive the grant of probate or letters of administration
- send an official copy of the grant to the bank, the insurance company, and so on, and get from them what belongs to the estate
- sell any property unless there are good reasons to postpone the sale
- pay the debts
- deal with outstanding income tax and CGT for the period up to the date of death and for the subsequent administration period (no CGT is payable upon death)
- pay the legacies; hand over the bequests
- distribute or invest the residue.

When to consult a solicitor

Any number of complexities can arise in connection with winding up an estate. Often the personal representatives are busy people, without the time to cope with the legal side of an administration and would not contemplate administering an estate without employing a solicitor.

In many cases, a solicitor's services are essential: when the deceased owned his own business, for instance, or was a partner in a firm, or was involved in an insurance syndicate, or where there is agricultural property, or when family trusts are involved (stemming from the deceased's parents, perhaps, or from a marriage settlement).

If the deceased left no will and the estate comes to more than £125,000 (after deducting the value of the personal effects including the car), the spouse will get the first £125,000 and a life interest in half the remainder provided that there are children as well, of whatever age. In this case, the complications likely to arise from the life interest make a solicitor's advice and help worthwhile. The same applies where, on an intestacy or under the will, some of the property is to pass to children who are at present under the age of 18. Their rights are called minority interests, and particular legal problems can arise regarding them. This is so whether the children are 17 weeks, 17 months or 17 years old.

Another situation which usually demands consulting a solicitor is where, on an intestacy, some long-forgotten relative is entitled to a share in the estate. For example, a brother may have gone to Australia forty years ago and not been heard of since. In such a case, the Australian brother is entitled, if the deceased left no will, to the same share as the sister who lovingly nursed the deceased through his last years of illness. The problems involved in tracing relatives who have apparently disappeared generally require careful handling, as does the situation if they are not, in fact, found.

Home-made wills, particularly on some of the printed forms, sometimes contain ambiguities or irregularities which can create difficulties, and legal help about the interpretation may be needed at some stage. An executor who wrongly interprets a will may become liable for the consequences of his mistake.

A solicitor should also be used if there is any possibility of anyone seeking a share, or a larger share, of the deceased's estate under the Inheritance (Provision for Family and Dependants) Act 1975, regardless of the terms of the will or the rules of intestacy.

If the estate is insolvent – if the debts exceed the value of the assets – a solicitor needs to be consulted. The same applies where, although the estate is solvent, there is not sufficient to pay all the legacies in full or there is no residue. (The solicitor's fees will be paid as one of the 'first claimants' against the assets in the estate, before other creditors.)

Solicitors' fees

A solicitor's fees for dealing with an estate are paid out of the deceased's property. They are a legitimate expense, like the funeral expenses and the IHT. The personal representatives do not have to pay them out of their own pockets; it is normally the residuary legatee who bears them, i.e. the person who, under the will, is to receive the rest of the deceased's property after paying out everything else, including these expenses.

There is no longer a recommended scale of fees for solicitors. The Law Society used to suggest, as a guide, the following as a basis for fees in normal probate cases: on a gross estate between £2,000 and £10,000, a rate of 3 per cent of the gross estate; on the next £40,000 (that is, between £10,000 and £50,000), 2½ per cent of the gross estate; lower rates applied above that.

Solicitors nowadays should charge fees in accordance with the Solicitors Remuneration Order 1972. This sets out the various elements that can affect the final fee, including the time spent, the complexity of the estate, and its value.

The charges should also be considerably less for a routine simple administration than for one in which complicated matters arise, although the solicitor will need to know if the estate has any serious difficulties. If the will states that a bank is to be the executor, it is worth confronting the bank at an early stage if you wish to challenge their costs as the banks still tend to calculate their charges according to a percentage of the gross estate. Typical charges would be 5 per cent of the first £75,000, with 3 per cent levied on the next £50,000, and 2 per cent on any balance over £125,000. If the estate is under £10,000, there is a minimum charge of £500 but there can be additional fees.

The Law Society tells solicitors that they should give their clients the 'best information possible' about the likely costs when they take instructions, so do remember to ask at an early stage if you are not told.

Do-it-yourself

There are precedents for people going about some enterprise which is generally the province of the legal profession. Some litigants in person, as they are called, have taken cases to court

Essential steps in probate administration

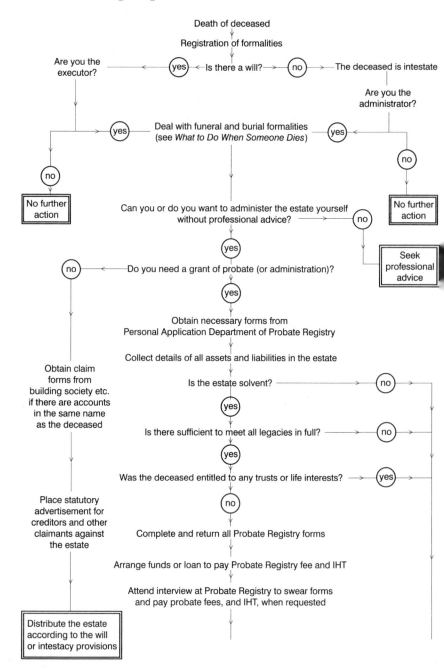

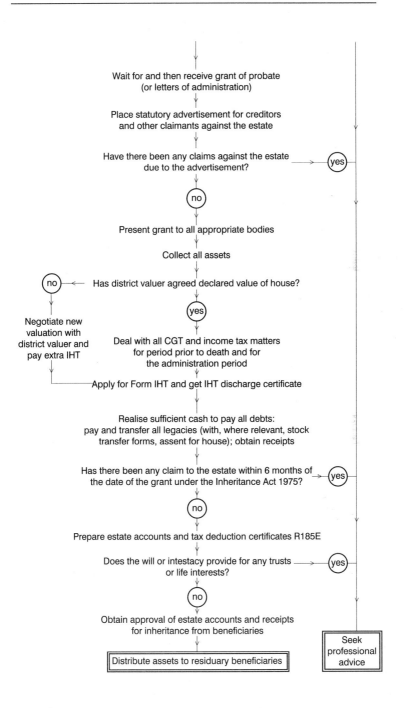

Wait for and then receive grant of probate
(or letters of administration)

Place statutory advertisement for creditors
and other claimants against the estate

Have there been any claims against the estate → yes
due to the advertisement?

no

Present grant to all appropriate bodies

Collect all assets

no ← Has district valuer agreed declared value of house?

yes

Negotiate new
valuation with
district valuer and
pay extra IHT

Deal with all CGT and income tax matters
for period prior to death and for
the administration period

Apply for Form IHT and get IHT discharge certificate

Realise sufficient cash to pay all debts:
pay and transfer all legacies (with, where relevant, stock
transfer forms, assent for house); obtain receipts

Has there been any claim to the estate within 6 months of → yes
the date of the grant under the Inheritance Act 1975?

no

Prepare estate accounts and tax deduction certificates R185E

Does the will or intestacy provide for any trusts → yes
or life interests?

no

Obtain approval of estate accounts and receipts
for inheritance from beneficiaries

Distribute assets to residuary beneficiaries

Seek
professional
advice

alone; many laymen have bought or sold a house without a solicitor. Whereas the litigant in person and the do-it-yourself house buyer must feel their way uncertainly through the same channels and procedures as lawyers, the personal representative will find that there is a special machinery set up just for him or her.

There is a Personal Application Department in each of the Probate Registries, which has special staff, forms and procedures designed to smooth the path of the inexperienced layman.

But the help and advice given by the Personal Application Department of a Probate Registry is confined to getting the grant of probate or letters of administration, and the personal representative is generally left to find out for himself or herself – by reading this book, for instance – what goes before and what comes after.

CHAPTER 6

THE ADMINISTRATION OF AN ESTATE

MARY Blake has died. Robert, her son, and Matthew Seaton, her son-in-law, are her executors. Matthew and Robert have agreed that they will not instruct a solicitor in connection with the administration of the estate.

Matthew is the businesslike member of the family, and it was natural that he took charge of events. Matthew had known of his appointment as one of the executors, but had never been shown the will itself. The will had been drawn up by a solicitor and put in the Blakes' deed box. If the will is lodged in the bank, the executor has to sign for it if he collects it in person, or acknowledge its safe receipt in writing if it is sent to him by post. Where several executors are named in the will, the bank may ask for all their signatures but should release the will to one of them on the understanding that in due course all the executors will sign an acknowledgement.

Sometimes the will may be held in a solicitor's office safe. There should be no need for the solicitor to keep the will, and he should release it to the executors against their signatures if they all sign a receipt for it. If he is also one of the executors it is difficult to exclude him but if his own firm is to deal with the administration of the estate make sure you are clear about the basis on which the firm will charge. If the solicitor who was appointed executor has left the firm concerned, or has retired, he must be contacted, but may be prepared to renounce as executor, leaving you free to administer the estate without reference to a firm of solicitors.

The date of Mary Blake's death was 8 April 1997.

Mary Blake's will

THIS IS THE LAST WILL AND TESTAMENT OF ME

MARY JOSEPHINE BLAKE of The Firs Willow Lane Minford Surrey Widow which I make this 16th day of August One thousand nine hundred and seventy two

1.   **I REVOKE** all earlier Wills

2.   **I APPOINT** as my Executors and Trustees my son Robert Anthony Blake of Wringapeak Farm Woody Bay Devon and my son-in-law Matthew John Seaton of 14 Twintree Avenue Minford Surrey

3.   (a) **I GIVE** my Diamond Brooch to my niece Barbara S. Forbes and the rest of my jewellery to my daughter Emma Seaton

(b) I give my Carriage Clock to my friend Josef Samson
(c) I give the sum of Fifty pounds (£50.00) to each of my grandchildren who shall be living at the date of my death
(d) I give the sum of One hundred pounds (£100.00) to Mrs Alison Ward of Rose Cottage Little Minford
(e) I give the sum of Two hundred pounds (£200.00) to Help the Aged of [address]
and declare that the receipt of a person who appears to be a proper officer of the Charity shall be a discharge to my Trustees
(f) I declare that the above mentioned gifts and bequests shall be paid free of any tax

Signed ....

Witness ....

Witness ....

[PAGE 2]

4.   **I GIVE** to my son Mark Douglas Blake free of any Inheritance Tax

(a) My freehold house known as 'The Firs' Willow Lane Minford Surrey and I direct that any mortgage or charge on my house at the date of my death shall be discharged out of my residuary estate
(b) Any car which I may own at the date of my death together with the contents of my home including all furniture and effects and personal belongings with the exception of the items mentioned at paragraph 3

5.   **MY TRUSTEES** shall hold the rest of my estate on trust to retain or sell it and:-

(a)   (i) To pay debts and executorship expenses

(ii) To pay any Inheritance Tax in respect of property passing under this Will

(b) To divide the residue equally between my daughter Emma Seaton and my son Robert Anthony Blake but if either of them should die before me without issue to pay the whole of it to the survivor

6.   IF ANY of my children should die before attaining a vested interest leaving children then those children shall on attaining Twenty One take equally between them any benefit under this Will which my deceased child would otherwise have taken

7.   MY TRUSTEES shall have the following power:-

(a) To invest as freely as if they were beneficially entitled

Signed ....

Witness ....

Witness ....

[PAGE 3]

(b) To apply actual assets rather than cash if they think fit without requiring the consent of any other person

9.   I EXPRESS A WISH that my body shall be cremated and my ashes scattered

IN WITNESS whereof I have hereunto set my hand on the date written at the beginning of this Will

SIGNED by the Testatrix in our   )
presence and attested by us in the   )
presence of the Testatrix and each   )
other:-   )

Matthew read the will at once to see what it said about burial or cremation. He had no intention of arranging a formal reading of the will to the family after the funeral. This ritual now happens mostly in the world of fiction. A beneficiary is not entitled to know the contents of the will until probate is granted, at which time the will becomes a public document. On the other hand, it does not have to be kept secret until then, and most executors are prepared to tell the main beneficiaries the extent of their benefit. But there is always the slight risk that the will might be found invalid for some reason, or a later will is found, or there is not enough in the estate to pay out all the legacies, so that no legacy can be positively confirmed until after probate is granted.

Mary Blake had been a widow; her will gave the main part of her estate to her three children, Emma, Robert and Mark. The first £215,000 of her estate would be immune from inheritance tax, but, with the exception of the charitable gift, the whole of the rest of the estate would be liable for tax.

She gave the house to Mark, who was unmarried and lived at home with her at the time of her death. The effect of the will was that any IHT due on the house, and the outstanding mortgage debt, were to be paid out of the estate – the residue of the estate, that is – so that Mark would inherit the house complete, without having to find any money to meet these liabilities. Had it not been for the specific direction in the will to this effect, he would have had to take the house subject to the mortgage on it.

The general rule is that the tax is borne by the residue, but that any charge on assets still binds the person who inherits them. For instance, if an overdraft had been secured by the deposit of shares with the bank, the person inheriting the shares, not the residuary legatee, has to settle the overdraft, unless the will or codicil says otherwise. (The testator might have added a codicil specifically to deal with this.)

However, it can be put into the will that this shall not apply in a particular case and that, for example, the proportion of tax attributable to the house should be borne by the person who inherits it. It is safest to state your wishes in regard to this quite clearly in your will.

First formalities

It is possible to arrange with the post office that for the period of, say, a year from the date of death all mail will be redirected to one of the executors. An application form for this can be obtained from any post office. A fee is payable depending on the number of months the service is needed. For one year it would come to around £30. But the fee can be repaid to the executor out of the estate in due course. This forwarding service is useful where, after a death, a house will be standing empty. In Matthew's case, he had a word with Mark who promised to send to him all his mother's mail. He also realised that he would have to check that the insurance on the house remained valid.

The first formality to be arranged was the registration of the death of Mrs Blake with the registrar of births, marriages and deaths. Once he had registered the death, Matthew was able to obtain copies of the various death certificates that would be needed on several occasions in the next few weeks.

In Mrs Blake's deed box Matthew found a number of other documents, including a life insurance policy, some National Savings certificates, a National Savings Bank book, a building society account book, some premium bonds and some share certificates. Matthew put them back into the box, together with the will, and took the box home.

From the contents of the will, Matthew had satisfied himself that he had full authority to act as an executor with his brother-in-law. Matthew's co-executor Robert, who lives in Devon, asked him to deal with the business side of the executorship, and left all the formalities to him. But Matthew made a point of specifically getting his brother-in-law to confirm in writing that this was so. Apart from the courtesy of doing so, this was legally the correct thing to do. Robert was as much an executor as he was, and the proper procedure was for both of them to authorise him to make the necessary arrangements on behalf of both of them. Moreover, both would need to sign all the various official papers because they were to be joint executors. Also, Robert should not forget that he is legally responsible for the proper administration of the estate along with Matthew.

Matthew and Robert were fully aware that the duties of an executor involved much work and a lot of responsibility. Executors are the people to whom the law looks to make sure that all the testator's wishes are carried out as far as is possible. They owe a duty of the utmost faith not only to the deceased but also to the creditors of the estate and the beneficiaries. They are under obligation to realise the maximum benefit from the estate and can be challenged by the beneficiaries or the creditors if there is any lapse from the highest standards of behaviour. They must therefore keep all matters of the administration of the estate entirely separate from their own personal affairs and be able to show, later on, by the preparation of estate accounts, that they have used no funds from the estate for their own personal purposes.

However, provided that they keep the necessary receipts and a separate note of the amounts involved, they are entitled to pay for minor items out of their own pockets and to recover these sums from the estate.

Executor not wishing to act

There may be a number of reasons why someone might wish to renounce his or her appointment as executor: for instance, a professional adviser who had not acted for the testator for a number of years, or a relative or friend who had had no contact with the testator for a long period, or simply someone who does not want to be troubled with the chore and responsibilities of the administration.

It is possible for either executor to renounce his or her right to take out a grant of probate.

A form of renunciation can be obtained from Oyez Stationery* (phone the head office for details of your nearest branch). Alternatively, at a later stage of the administration, the probate office will send the appropriate piece of paper, called a power reserved letter, for the renouncing executor to sign.

If one of the executors renounces, the substitute (if one is named in the will) automatically comes in, unless he or she also renounces.

It is possible for a person named as executor in the will to appoint an attorney for the purpose of obtaining the grant; the attorney then acts as if he or she had actually been named as the executor in the will. (The appropriate form for this can be obtained from the Oyez shops.)

It is also possible for a personal representative who has obtained a grant to appoint an attorney to act for him or her in the rest of the administration. Usually the power lasts for one year and relieves a personal representative of the form-signing part of the administration. It is often useful where the executor is abroad. (Since 1985 there have been rules enabling an attorney to act during the incapacity of some people and in some cases this can cover the incapacity of an executor. The rules are complicated, and, if any question of incapacity through old age or mental illness arises, you should seek legal advice.)

Matthew and Robert each knew quite a lot about Mary Blake's affairs and both were interested in dealing with the administration, so there was no doubt in their minds that they should proceed, as quickly as possible, to obtain the grant and act in the administration themselves.

Mary Blake's estate

Within a few days, Matthew had assembled most of the available documents regarding the late Mary Blake's property. He opened a large file with different sections for each organisation he would need to contact (bank, insurance company, etc.) so that he would have an immediately accessible record of all the correspondence, both letters to him and copies of his own, and avoid getting in a muddle.

He took a copy of the will for this file, keeping the will itself in a drawer safely away from hole punches, staples and other office paraphernalia that might render it void.

He then started to prepare a list of all the items, with an estimate of the value of each. He was able, from the documents he had found in the house, together with information from his relatives, to compile a provisional list of the assets that made up the estate, making an estimate where he was doubtful.

		approximately
Provisional details of Mary Blake's estate		£
Building Society account, Rockley B. S.		16,500
National Savings Bank account (plus interest to date of death)		400
National Savings certificates (500 units)		700
premium bonds		1,500
various stocks and shares (to be valued, but say approximately)		60,000
house: The Firs, Willow Lane, Minford	125,000	
less outstanding mortgage	25,000	
		100,000
anticipated proceeds of mortgage life endowment policy with Immortal Life Assurance Society		38,500
3 paintings by well-known artists		11,500
other contents (including furniture)		1,000
car		1,350
wedding ring and other jewellery		1,500
bank account: Barminster Bank (about)		200
Bridstow life insurance policy (plus profits)		8,500
balance of pensions to date of death		50
other odds and ends, say		300
approximate gross estate		£242,000

debts		
funeral	1,200	
miscellaneous, say	200	
		1,400
approximate net estate		£240,600
IHT (approx.)		10,240
		230,360
probate fees and other expenses		1,000
approximate value to divide according to will		229,360
say		230,000

He left a column at the right-hand side blank so that he could fill in the real figures alongside the estimates as they became known. He put this provisional list of assets right at the front of the file for easy access.

Valuation of assets

Matthew now had a good idea of what was likely to be involved in administering the estate. He would have to write to the bank manager, the building society, and the insurance company, etc., to find out the precise value of some of the assets, along the following lines:

Dear Sir,

Re: Mary Josephine Blake deceased

I am an executor of the will of the late Mary Josephine Blake, who died on 8 April 1997. My co-executor is her son, Robert Anthony Blake of Wringapeak Farm, Woody Bay, Devon.

The estate includes the asset described below. Please let me know the value of this asset at the date of death, together with any accrued interest.

I enclose the relevant death certificate. When the grant of probate has been obtained, I shall send an official copy of it to you for your inspection. Please let me know what formalities (if any) will be involved in obtaining payment of what is due to the estate.

Particulars of asset:
Name in which held:
Description of asset:
Reference number:
Estimated amount of value: £
Additional information:

Yours faithfully,

Various National Savings

Matthew obtained a claim form DNS 904 (Death of a holder of National Savings) from a post office and entered full details of the late saver, Mary Josephine Blake, and of her National Savings.

He confirmed on the form that none of these savings was held jointly or in trust and that Mary Josephine Blake had left a will for which he intended to obtain a grant of probate, and that he was an executor. He could indicate on the form whether he wished to keep assets in National Savings or have the money repaid. There were quite a number of National Savings certificate books among Mrs Blake's papers, some going back many years, containing printed certificates from several of the various issues of savings certificates that have been made over the years, and some of the new certificates with a computerised holder's number. Matthew prepared a list on a separate sheet of paper attached it, because there was not enough room on the form, setting out the savings certificates individually, specifying the cost of each certificate, the number of units represented by it, the serial number on the certificate, and the date of its issue, found by reference to the circular date stamp or computer-printed date on it.

There are various addresses listed on the form to which the completed form could be sent, depending on the types of savings involved. Because there was a National Savings Bank account among Mary Blake's property, he sent the completed form to the Department for National Savings* in Glasgow. That office would arrange for the other National Savings assets to be dealt with. With the form, he sent the securities themselves (bank book, savings certificates, premium bonds).

Valuations of these various assets would be sent to Matthew from the offices concerned together with repayment/transfer forms, depending on how he had indicated the assets were to be dealt with.

The premium bonds did not need to have an official valuation. They retain their face value and no question of interest arises. They could not be nominated and cannot be transferred to beneficiaries, but may be left in the ERNIE prize draws for twelve calendar months following the death, and then cashed. The money can be reinvested in new bonds in the name of the beneficiary, but these will have to wait three months before becoming eligible for inclusion in the prize draw. National Savings should be notified of the bondholder's death as soon as possible. Any prizes received after the bondholder's death should be returned to the Bonds and Stock Office for them to determine and confirm that the deceased's estate is eligible and entitled to receive it. Where it happens that a prize warrant has been paid into the deceased's bank account after the date of death but before either the bank or the Bonds Office has been notified to freeze the account or stop payment, the Bonds and Stock Office will ask for the prize to be returned so that a new warrant can be sent to the executors after probate has been registered.

Where the value of all National Savings accounts or bonds (including interest and any premium bond prize won since the date of death) is £5,000 or less, they may normally be paid out without any grant having been obtained. National Savings may, however, ask if a grant is being obtained, and if so may refuse to pay without sight of it, unless the savings were nominated or held jointly or in trust.

Bank accounts

Mary Blake did not have a Girobank account. When a Girobank account holder dies, his account is administered according to the rules of ordinary banking practice.

Matthew knew that his mother-in-law had kept an account at the Minford branch of the Barminster Bank. He found the cheque book, the paying-in book and the bank statements in a drawer in the house. When a bank is given notice of a customer's death, cheques drawn on that account are returned unpaid with a note 'drawer deceased', and all standing orders or direct debit mandates cease. Any cheques drawn by the deceased but not met on presentation because of notice of death having been lodged at the bank should be regarded as a debt due from the deceased to the payee. (Plastic cards should be cut in half, so that they cannot be used fraudulently.) If any payments are to be made to the account, the amounts will be held by the bank in a suspense account for the time being.

Normally, a bank must not disclose to other people the details of how much is in a customer's account and what securities, deeds or other papers or articles are held, let alone hand them over. The exception is where the information is needed by the executors or administrators after a death, so that the inheritance tax accounts can be completed.

Matthew wrote a letter to the bank manager of the Minford branch, concluding with these details:

Particulars of asset:
Name in which held: Mary Josephine Blake
Description of asset: current account
Reference number: 00860727
Estimated amount or value: unknown
Additional information required: please let me know
1. whether Mrs Blake kept a deposit account at your branch and, if so, the balance at the date of death and the interest accrued to the date of death but not yet added to the account
2. whether she kept a deed box at your branch, or otherwise deposited any documents or other property with you.

He also asked the bank to let him know the details of standing orders, direct debits and so on that his mother-in-law had had so that he could decide whether any further steps were necessary. For instance, if she had had a direct debit arrangement for her gas supply he would write to the gas company explaining that she had died and that therefore the standing order would cease, and letting them know that he would settle the payment when the house was transferred to its new owner.

Joint bank account

When assets are held in joint names, it is necessary to fix a value on the share that belonged to the joint owner who died. In the case of a joint bank account, for instance, the executors might sometimes have to find out the source of the money paid to the credit of the account, as this indicates the proportions in which the credit balance on the date of death was held. Where both joint holders contributed from their own money to the joint account, it is necessary to identify payments into the account over a period of years, and to calculate the respective total contributions to the account. The credit balance at the date of death would then be divided between the joint account holders in those proportions. If it is impossible to show who contributed what, or if the items in the account are too numerous or complicated to make it possible to distinguish the sources, the balance is considered to be held equally by its joint holders.

However, where the two joint account holders are husband and wife, it is presumed, even if all the money came only from the husband or only from the wife, that it is held by them equally. Therefore, half the balance on the date of death is taken as the value belonging to the person who has died. Circumstances may also show that a joint account held by an unmarried couple is owned equally between the joint account holders.

This information is needed merely in order to establish how much of the money in the bank has to be included in the IHT returns, not in order to decide how much the survivor can draw from the account. After death, the survivor is usually entitled to the whole of the balance and can continue to use the account straight away because it is not frozen – unlike other accounts.

A joint account has the advantage that the survivor can continue to draw on the account, even though the other account holder has died. As it can take weeks, even months, to get a grant of probate, this allows the survivor to have continued access to ready cash. The balance to the credit of a joint account passes automatically to the survivor and so bypasses the will (unless it is a trust account or some specific other agreement was made between the joint account holders), but is counted in for calculating inheritance tax (even though none will be payable if the survivor is the spouse). If there is enough money in the account, the money can be used to pay inheritance tax, provided the co-owner of the bank account is the residuary beneficiary.

With any assets held jointly – building society accounts, savings bank accounts and investments, for instance – similar principles apply.

Building society account
Matthew had found the Rockley Building Society passbook and in it was the address of the branch where the account was orig-

inally opened. He wrote to the manager of the branch, so that a note of the death could be made on the passbook, to ensure there was no possibility of some fraudulent person making withdrawals on the account. With the letter, he sent the passbook. The amount shown in the book might not necessarily be the current balance of the account because there may have been further payments in, or withdrawals via the card-machine. He therefore added the following paragraph to his letter:

> I shall be grateful if you will let me known the capital balance standing to the credit of the account at the date of death, and a note of all interest accrued due but not added to the account at that date.

Life insurance

Matthew also wrote a letter of enquiry to the Bridstow Insurance Company. He had found a life assurance policy with that company among the documents in the deed box. It provided for the payment of £8,000 on Mary Blake's death. Matthew found that it was a with-profits policy, which meant that in addition to the £8,000 to be paid to the executors by the insurance company, a further amount would be paid. In the letter to the local branch manager of the insurance company, Matthew gave the following particulars:

> Particulars of asset:
> Name in which held: Mary Josephine Blake
> Description of asset: whole life insurance, issued 14 June 1972
> Reference number: policy HPX 941/37
> Estimated amount or value: over £8,000
> Additional information required: as this policy was with-profits, please let me know the amount payable in addition to the sum assured.

Matthew had now set in train the procedure for valuing the property left by his mother-in-law. Even where he knew, or had a fair idea of, the value of an asset, he still asked the organisation concerned for a written valuation, in case he should need evidence of the value of any item.

Valuation of the house

Matthew now turned his attention to the question of valuing the house. Most people have some idea of the current value of the houses in their locality. It is not essential in the first instance to obtain a professional valuation from a firm of surveyors and valuers.

Whether you have a professional valuation or not, your figure will be checked sooner or later by an official called the district valuer. He is employed by the Inland Revenue, but his job has little to do with taxes as such. He is concerned with the valuation of land, houses, factories, shops, offices and so on, for many official purposes. He is an expert on valuation, so there is no point in trying to understate the value of a house. However, for possible saving on IHT, you may as well put down your lowest estimate of value. A point which can be made is that the value is lower because for IHT purposes one has to take the value on a particular day, so it is as if one had to effect a forced sale on that day. The district valuer will query your figure later on if it is too low, but perhaps not if it is on the high side. As there is IHT to pay on the estate, Matthew might be wise to bring in a professional valuer to prepare a valuation as he could then argue the case with the district valuer if it were challenged.

However (particularly in an estate where there is no inheritance tax payable), stating a higher value could mean less tax in the long run if there is a danger that any future sale might be subject to capital gains tax. The value for IHT is the beneficiary's base cost for CGT purposes, so a low IHT value might mean a larger gain on any future sale. (Usually the private residence CGT exemption will apply, but this is not invariably the case.)

Matthew estimated the value of The Firs at £125,000. Where a house is not going to be sold it is possible to agree a value for the house with the district valuer before applying for probate, but this can delay matters, and anyhow Matthew did not know whether Mark would want to keep or sell the house, so he went ahead and estimated the value as realistically as he could.

If the house was joint property
There are two different ways in which property may be held jointly: as joint tenants or as tenants-in-common. Property is usually conveyed to married couples as joint tenants and to business partners as tenants-in-common, but you can choose which you want.

Where a house is owned by joint tenants, the share of the first to die passes to the survivor automatically on death. The survivor of joint tenants acquires the other half-share, in fact, merely by surviving, irrespective of anything the will may say. The terms of the deceased's will do not apply to it at all. In the case of tenants-in-common, however, the share of the first to die forms part of the estate; that share may, of course, pass to the spouse (or whoever is the co-owner) under the will, but that is not the same thing as passing to him or her automatically, as happens when it is a joint tenancy, and it may go to someone quite different. Whenever a house is held in the joint names of a husband and wife (or any two people), when one of them dies, the value of his or her share has to be declared for IHT purposes.

It can make a difference to the value of a share in a jointly held house whether it was held as joint tenants or as tenants-in-common. That would be the first thing for the executor to find out (from the deeds and documents) in the process of valuing the share in a house, on the death of one of the joint owners.

If it was held as tenants-in-common, the executor will have to know the proportions in which it was held in order to estimate the value of the share of the deceased at the date of death. Although it is often held in equal shares, this is not always so. If held as joint tenants, it will automatically be half and half (or equal shares if there are more than two joint tenants).

The vacant possession value at the date of death is the starting point in calculating the value of the deceased's share of the house for IHT. Suppose it is the figure of £60,000. In the case of a joint tenancy or a tenancy-in-common held in equal shares, that figure must be divided by two, to allow for the share of only the one who died; this would give a figure of £30,000.

But this is not yet the true net value of the deceased's share. Because it was only a share in a house, and because the other joint owner still has the right to live there, it follows that the deceased's share must be worth less than precisely half of the full value; the value is reduced by the very fact that someone can still live there. For IHT, value means the price a buyer would pay in the open market on the day of death. It is hardly likely that a buyer (if one could be found) would pay as much as half of the vacant possession price for a half-share, when there is a stranger still living in the house.

The result is that the proper value of the half-share (in the case of a tenancy-in-common held in equal shares) is half the vacant possession value, less something for the mere fact of its being held jointly. The £30,000 for half the vacant possession value might well be depressed by about 15 per cent to £25,500 on this account. There is no rigid formula that applies to this aspect of the valuation, and it is difficult to arrive at a figure because, in practice, shares in jointly owned houses are hardly ever sold. Nevertheless, the expert valuer should be able to decide on a figure. Some valuation officers do not readily accept this basis of the value of the share in a house held by the deceased jointly with someone else, but it is correct. And sometimes valuation officers do not accept any reduction for the 'forced sale' factor. But a hypothetical valuation such as this cannot, in any case, be absolutely accurate and a tolerance of 15 per cent either way is usually regarded by valuers as acceptable. In cases like this the cost of engaging a professional valuer should be covered by the better result he should achieve in negotiations with the district valuer.

When the property is owned jointly by husband and wife, valuation officers do not then allow any such reduction in the value because of what is called 'related property' provisions which apply under the Inheritance Tax Act. However, if before the death the property was jointly owned by, say, brothers and sisters, or two or more friends, or parent and child, or any two people not married to each other, it is worth arguing for a reduction in the valuation. Where the surviving co-owner of the property is the husband or wife, the value will have to be half the value of the whole house.

The situation can arise when the property is in the sole name of the spouse or other person who had died and the non-owner survivor claims that he or she has a beneficial interest in the property in his or her own right, so that only the deceased's share in the property would need to be declared for IHT purposes. Legal advice should be taken in such a case.

Account must also be taken of any mortgage debt outstanding. Suppose that it is £2,000; then the deceased's share of this debt would normally be half, that is £1,000. The result would be that the value of the deceased's share of the house less the mortgage debt would be £25,500 minus £1,000, that is £24,500.

Matthew was not involved in the problem of valuing a share in a house jointly held, because he knew that the house was in Mrs Blake's name alone. If Matthew had been uncertain whether the house was in her name alone or a joint ownership and there was no declaration of trust or other evidence of joint ownership among Mrs Blake's documents, he would have to ask the building society that held the title deeds.

The outstanding mortgage

There was a mortgage on the house, on which there was about £25,000 to be paid, according to a statement from the building society which Matthew had found in Mrs Blake's papers. The statement gave the position as it was on the previous 1 July, and it would be necessary, Matthew knew, to obtain an exact figure showing the position at the date of his mother-in-law's death. He wrote this letter to the building society:

[Date]

Dear Sir,

Re: Mary Josephine Blake deceased

I am an executor of the will of the late Mary Josephine Blake, who died on 8 April 1997; my co-executor is her son, Robert Anthony Blake. I enclose the relevant death certificate.

Mrs Blake owned the house where she lived: The Firs, Willow Lane, Minford, on which there is an outstanding mortgage with your society. The reference number is AME716. Please let me know exactly how much capital was outstanding on the mortgage at the date of death, and also the amount of interest due up to that date.

Could you also please advise me of the amount to be paid under the Immortal Life Assurance Society endowment policy which should show a slight surplus over the amount required for the repayment of the mortgage. Please let me know what formalities there are in this respect and send the claim form for completion.

I do not appear to have any record of the date on which the mortgage was made. Please let me know this.

Yours faithfully,

There had been little discussion so far about whether Mrs Blake's son Mark, to whom she had left the house in her will, would continue to live there, or whether it would be sold. What was to happen eventually could be decided later on. It would have to be Mark's decision, once the administration was all completed. But the decision could not be made until then, in case there were some heavy debts to pay which were not yet known about. If such debts were to amount to more than the residue of the estate, the property could have to be sold to pay for these even though it had been specifically left to him in the will.

Shares

In this section of the book, the company names have been taken merely to illustrate the workings of administering an estate, to give an air of reality. The prices and dividends, and other figures, are in no way intended to reflect the actual performance of the shares or the companies over the period covered.

Matthew next turned his attention to the question of finding out the value of another item which made up his mother-in-law's property: the shares.

In the deed box, together with the will, Matthew had found the share certificates for the various holdings, namely:

    389 ordinary shares in Alliance Trust plc
    390 ordinary shares in Unilever plc
    247 ordinary shares in Monks Investment Trust plc
    440 ordinary shares in BAT Industries plc
    1,890 ordinary 25p shares in Shell Transport and Trading plc
    2,150 ordinary 25p shares in Coats Viyella plc
    180 ordinary shares in Marks & Spencer plc
    3,000 ordinary 25p shares in British Telecom plc
    3,000 ordinary 25p shares in British Gas plc
    15,000 ordinary 25p shares in Stonehill Holdings plc
    3,500 Allied Dunbar Japan Fund Units.

Matthew had already made a rough calculation of what those items were worth on the date of death, by looking up the closing prices in the paper. Now it became necessary to work it out exactly, and in accordance with the accepted formula for valuing shares for IHT. This formula applies to shares which are bought and sold on the London Stock Exchange, and which are therefore quoted there. The shares of all the well-known large companies, and a great number of others as well, are quoted on the London Stock Exchange, as are war stock and numerous other government securities and similar investments, but not defence bonds.

On any particular day, there are sales of shares in nearly all the big concerns, and the prices often vary, depending on the prevailing circumstances. At any one time two prices are quoted – the higher is that at which people buy and the lower at which people sell. The closing prices are the two prevailing prices of the share at the time in the afternoon when the Stock Exchange closed dealing for the day; they are usually different from the highest or the lowest price at which the shares were quoted on that day.

The value of the holding

To work out the value which is officially recognised for probate purposes, it is necessary to know the closing prices on the day of the deceased's death. The *Stock Exchange Daily Official List* gives the closing prices, the required figures, in a concise way. If the death was at the weekend, prices from the official list for the Friday or for the Monday may be used, and the executor may mix the Friday and Monday prices to his (that is, the estate's) advantage.

Not many people have ready access to the *Stock Exchange Daily Official List*. The local reference library may take it, and a very large branch of a bank may take it. If you telephone your bank manager, quoting the securities you wish to value, he will be able to find out and let you know the closing prices for each share for the date of the death in question. If there is a long list, it is probably better to write to the bank. Alternatively, a stockbroker would be able to provide this information quite easily, either on the telephone in the case of a few quotations, or by letter if there are more. When a stockbroker makes a valuation his charge is based on a percentage of the value of the shares.

Anyone can obtain back copies of the *Stock Exchange Daily Official List* for a relatively small sum – contact FT Information Ltd* for details.

Matthew decided to buy a copy of the official list to make the valuation. It arrived within five days. He found that six of the companies in which he was interested were quoted in the section of the *Daily Official List* headed 'Commercial, Industrial'; the Shell and British Gas shares were classified as being 'Oil and Gas'; if there had been any government stock it would have been classified under British Funds; other stocks would have an appropriate listing under Corporation and County stocks.

In each case, Matthew found the price quoted. He was then able to adopt the official formula to work out the value of each for probate purposes. The formula is this: take as the figure a price which is one quarter up from the lower to the higher figure. If the two figures in the quotation column of the *Stock Exchange Daily Official List* are, for instance 100p and 104p, then you take 101p as the value; if the two prices are 245p and 255p, then you take 247.5p as the value. The prices quoted in the official list are often prices for every £1 share held; the nominal value of a share may be 20p, 25p, £1, or any one of many other amounts.

Matthew prepared a complete table showing the share values. The shares turned out to be worth, on the date of death, £69,378.08 – considerably more than his first estimate.

amount held	description	prices quoted	¹/₄ up from lower	value of holding
		p	p	£
389	25p Alliance Trust	2267–2307	2277	8,857.53
390	25p Unilever plc	1376–1396	1381	5,385.90
247	25p Monks Investment	612–624	615	1,519.05
440	25p BAT Industries plc	441–481	451	1,984.40
1,890	25p Shell Transport plc	994–1010	998	18,862.20
2,150	25p Coats Viyella plc	136–144	138	2,967.00
180	25p Marks & Spencer plc	484–508	490	882.00
3,000	25p British Telecom plc	367–371	368	11,040.00
3,000	25p British Gas plc	229–237	231	6,930.00
15,000	25p Stonehill Holdings plc	72–76 xd	73	10,950.00
				£69,378.08

xd = ex-dividend price

Matthew wanted to check that he had got the holdings of the shares correct. There might have been rights issues for which his mother-in-law had not yet received the certificates, for example. So he wrote a letter to the registrar of each company concerned. The address of the registrar usually appears on the counterfoil of the dividend warrant. The counterfoil also acts as a certificate of income tax paid so people usually keep it in a safe place, but an executor cannot always find the counterfoils for all share holdings simply because the deceased may not have kept them or they may be at the bank if the dividends were credited there directly from the company or they may be at the deceased's accountants. There is a book called the *Register of Registrars*, kept in some reference libraries, which gives details of the registrar of each company quoted on the Stock Exchange, or you could telephone the head office of the companies concerned to find the proper address to write to, for the registrar. Quite often the 'registrar' is another company such as 'Lloyds Bank Registrars Ltd' or 'National Westminster Registration Services Ltd'. (The registrar for government stocks would be the Accountant General at the Bank of England's head office; for other stocks it would be the appropriate registrar's department or finance department.) The full address for the Allied Dunbar unit trusts was given in the unit trust information columns of *The Times*.

The letter he wrote was as follows:

[Date]

Dear Sir,

The estate of Mary Josephine Blake deceased Holding of .... Company ....
I am one of the joint executors of the estate of my mother-in-law who died on 8 April 1997. The only other executor is my brother-in-law, the deceased's son.

I enclose a copy of the death certificate for noting in your records. I am in the course of preparing the papers for the grant of probate and among the deceased's papers I have found the certificates for the above holding. I shall be grateful if you will confirm to me the holding as above registered in the deceased's name, and also confirm to me that there are no unclaimed dividend or interest payments held at your offices.

I look forward to hearing from you as soon as possible so that I can finalise the probate papers.

Yours faithfully,

Matthew had now set about valuing all the securities he had been able to find belonging to his mother-in-law on the date of her death. (He knew that he would later have to account to the Inland Revenue for income tax on any income from the securities which he received while he was administering the estate.)

Unit trusts

If you own shares in one company, you do not know how well that company is going to perform and therefore what profits it will earn, which directly affects the value of the shares. Many people consider it useful to spread the risk, by owning shares in a number of larger companies.

Some investment managers have specialised in this and it is possible to buy units in a pool of investments where the investment managers specifically aim to spread the risk and avoid loss. With unit trusts, you do not buy and sell specific shares in companies but buy and sell a specific number of units. This 'unit trust' industry is itself very specialised; investment managers now specialise in different funds so that units can be bought in a portfolio consisting, for example, of property companies, of industrial companies, or of electrical companies.

Matthew noted that his mother-in-law had a certificate for Allied Dunbar unit trust; Allied Dunbar, in this case, are the trust fund managers. The certificate was for units in their 'Japan Fund' and this means that the money is held invested in a wide spread of companies quoted on the Japanese Stock Exchange.

In his letter to Allied Dunbar Unit Trusts Matthew asked the trust manager to confirm the closing prices on the date of his mother-in-law's death and the value of the holding. Their reply in due course gave this as £5,715.50; Matthew filled in the list of assets accordingly.

Private companies

Although older 'Ltd' certificates are still quite valid, all companies whose shares are quoted on the Stock Exchange are now registered with the words 'Public Limited Company' or 'plc' at the end of the name. Private companies, whose shares are not quoted on the Stock Exchange (and which cannot be freely sold) all have the word 'Limited' or 'Ltd' at the end of their name.

Valuing shares in a private company not quoted on the Stock Exchange requires expert help, as a rule. Sometimes the secretary or accountant of the company concerned can state the price at which shares have recently changed hands, and this may be accepted for probate purposes. If not, a detailed and possibly difficult negotiation of value may have to be undertaken, and unless the shares are of comparatively small value, it would be worthwhile to get a lawyer or an accountant to handle the matter. The basis of valuation is different depending upon whether the interest in the company is a minority or a majority shareholding.

Ex-dividend

Matthew noticed that the price for Stonehill Holdings plc had the letters 'xd' beside it, which means that the price was quoted 'ex-dividend'. This means that if the shares are sold, the seller will receive the next dividend on these shares, not the buyer. The price the buyer pays is therefore lower than he would otherwise pay, to the extent of the dividend he is forgoing. This is because the company prepares the actual dividend cheques in advance in favour of the owner at that time, so if the shares are sold before the company sends out the cheque on the day the dividend is due, it will still go to the seller. This usually happens about six weeks before the date for payment of dividends.

In this case, the share's price went ex-dividend on 22 March 1997, so Matthew made a note to expect a dividend cheque in May. Because the price does not therefore reflect the full value of the shares, the dividend must be included as another asset in Matthew's list. By phoning the registrar of the company, he found out that the dividend to be paid on the shares was 1.715p each, so he calculated that the dividend would be £257.25. This would have to be included as a separate asset in the Inland Revenue account of Mary Blake's estate.

Pensions

Matthew found the papers relating to the pension scheme operated by his late father-in-law's former employers. It was a contributory pension scheme under which he had received a pension until his death and which then provided a pension, of half the amount, for Mrs Blake for the rest of her life. There was only one point arising which was strictly relevant to the administration of Mrs Blake's estate: the proportion of the month's pension due up to the date of her death. Matthew wrote to the secretary of the pension fund:

Dear Sir,

Re: Mary Josephine Blake deceased

You will be sorry to hear that Mrs Blake of The Firs, Willow Lane, Minford, died on 8 April 1997. I enclose a copy of the death certificate. As you know, she was receiving a widow's pension from the fund administered by you.

Her son, Mr Robert Anthony Blake, is one of the executors of her will, and I am the other. Please let me know the amount of Mrs Blake's pension due up to the date of her death.

Please also confirm that no capital sum is due to the estate under your pension scheme.

Yours faithfully,

Employers' occupational pension schemes, which provide for the payment of a pension to a former member of the company's staff, vary in form and detail. Many are based on the employee's final salary; in some, the pension is calculated according to the contributions made to the pension fund by the company and by the member during the years in which he or she was employed by the company. This had been the basis of the pension which Herbert Blake had been receiving during his years of retirement. The scheme then went on to provide for the payment of a further pension to the widow of a pensioner, this being a proportion (in this case half) of the earlier pension. In these circumstances, no other payment, such as a capital payment to the executors, was due under the scheme.

Quite often a pension scheme provides that a capital sum should become payable on the death of one of its members. For instance, if a member were to die while still an employee, that is before retirement, the scheme might provide for the return of the contributions which had been made over the years by the member, and from which he has, in the event, derived no benefit, because he did not survive to collect his pension. If the lump sum that represents this return of contributions were part of the deceased's estate, it would have to be declared for IHT. However, in most schemes nowadays it would be paid 'at the trustees' discretion' and not be subject to IHT. Such schemes provide that the trustees may select who is to receive the capital sum (but they are bound by the rules of the particular scheme, and some are quite restrictive). They may pay it all to the widow or they may share it between any number of dependants or pay it to the executors as part of the estate. If they pay it to the widow or to the dependants, the money forms no part of the deceased's estate. As a result, the discretionary payment to a widow or dependant is not subject to IHT.

Whatever the circumstances, it is probably best, where the deceased belonged to a pension scheme, to get a letter from the secretary of the pension fund to confirm the exact position regarding what the estate (as distinct from a dependant) is entitled to receive under the scheme. Even if it is only the proportion of the pension due for the last few days of life, a letter should be obtained to provide written confirmation for the purpose of IHT.

State benefits

Matthew's mother-in-law had also been receiving the state old age pension, or National Insurance retirement pension as it is properly called. Matthew found the pension book and noticed that she had not drawn her pension for the week in which she died.

Any arrears of pension, as well as the full pension for the week in which death took place, is paid to the executors after probate has been obtained, if they claim it. Pensions are paid on a specified day each week, for the week ahead. If a person collected the pension on Thursday and then dies on the following Monday, his estate would not be liable to refund any part of that week's pension. Where a person received the pension monthly or quarterly in arrears, or had it paid direct into a bank account, the death should be reported to the local office of the Department of Social Security who will adjust the payment accordingly.

Matthew sent off his mother-in-law's pension book. The sum due for arrears of pension formed part of Mrs Blake's estate; it would have to be declared for IHT and included in the probate papers.

Consumers' Association's book, *What to Do When Someone Dies,* includes a detailed account of National Insurance allowances and pensions that may be due after a death, and how to obtain them.

A payment can be claimed from the state (via an application to the Social Fund) to cover the reasonable cost of a funeral only if the person responsible for it is in receipt of Income Support, or Family Credit or Housing Benefit.

Income tax

Income tax is calculated on a person's total income in the tax year, 6 April to 5 April. PAYE works so that tax is deducted week by week, or month by month, on the assumption that the tax-payer will go on having income throughout the year. If he dies during the year, the PAYE assumptions are upset, because the taxpayer did not live to receive the income throughout the tax year, and often a tax repayment is due. Also, if the taxpayer was not liable for tax at the standard rate, because his income did not reach that level, there may be entitlement to a tax repayment if some of his income is taxed at the standard rate before he gets it; dividends from shares fall within this category. Personal repre-sentatives should explain the situation fully to the local inspec-tor of taxes, and if necessary go to see him about the repayment that may be due because too much income tax was levied on the deceased during the tax year in which he died. Although tax is claimed only on the amount of income received up to the date of death, tax allowances (such as a single person's or a married man's personal allowance) are granted for the full year, even if, as here, the death takes place early in the tax year. If Mrs Blake had an accountant, Matthew might find it more convenient to ask him to complete her tax returns to the date of her death.

Now Matthew wrote to the local inspector of taxes.

[Date]

Dear Sir,

Re: Mary Josephine Blake deceased

The tax affairs of the above-named have, I believe, been dealt with in your district, under reference B 246537. Mrs Blake of The Firs, Willow Lane, Minford, died on 8 April 1997. Her son Robert Anthony Blake, of Wringapeak Farm, Woody Bay, Devon, and I are the executors of her will, and we are in the process of applying for a grant of probate.

The only income which Mrs Blake was receiving up to the date of her death consisted of: pension from her late husband's former employers' pension fund (which was paid subject to PAYE); her state retirement pension; interest from a building society account from which tax is regarded as having already been deducted, and dividends from various investments. I enclose a list of them showing the dividends received from 6 April 1996 to 5 April 1997 and the one dividend (Coats Viyella) she has so far received in the current tax year 1996–7. There may be a repayment due to Mrs Blake in respect of PAYE deducted (and dividends taxed by deduction at 20%) for the period up to the date of her death in the current tax year.

If there is any information you require from me, please let me know.

I shall need to know the amount of the repayment for probate purposes, so I look forward to hearing from you.

Yours faithfully,

Contents of house and cash

The next item requiring valuation was the furniture and effects. This includes furniture in the house, household goods of all kinds, jewellery, clothes, a car and all personal possessions. It is not necessary to prepare a complete list, nor to state the respective values of different kinds of articles; they can all be lumped together.

Where the person who has died was sharing the house with a husband (or wife) or any other person, it is important to realise that it is only the deceased's household goods, effects, furniture and so on which need to be included in any valuation for tax purposes. A husband and wife may have regarded all of the property as being jointly owned by the two of them so that, on the death of either, they all become wholly owned by the survivor. In this case, one-half of the value of all the contents should be included. If the deceased owned any particular items outright, the full value of those items will have to be included. (There may be specific items bought by the husband or the wife particularly for himself/herself, or acquired by way of inheritance from their own respective families. Such items could quite possibly have been regarded by them as the one's or the other's individual property, not owned by the two of them jointly.) The executors should discuss the matter with the other person concerned, to ascertain precisely what was owned by the deceased, what was owned by the other person, and what was owned jointly.

It will usually be assumed that, as between husband and wife, the items are owned jointly. If property is jointly owned, it will become owned by the surviving owner regardless of the provisions of the will or intestacy although part of the value will have to be declared for tax purposes. But as between other people, for example an unmarried couple, it is usually assumed that the person who paid for an item owns it. Obviously, the provisions in a will (or indeed, intestacy) can operate only on the property which is found to be part of the deceased's estate and no tax is payable on anything owned by someone else.

The make and age of the car are the principal factors which affect its value; its condition is a minor consideration. A study of the prices being asked for second-hand cars by local garages or dealers will give an indication of the value, to within about £50. Do not forget to deduct any outstanding loan. If the car is on hire purchase, contact the hire purchase company to obtain their consent to sale.

The remaining articles are not so easily valued. It is better to put a separate valuation on items of particular value, such as things worth more than about £100, when making a calculation of the total value of the effects. This might apply, for example, to a particular piece of jewellery, or a picture, especially if its value is reasonably well established, perhaps because it was recently purchased or had been valued recently by an expert for insurance.

Matthew was not sure whether any of his mother-in-law's jewellery was worth a lot. He put into a box her wedding ring, a gold watch, several necklaces, one of which seemed to be made of gold with a ruby pendant, a pearl tie-pin (perhaps itself an heirloom) and the diamond brooch mentioned in the will. The local jeweller made a list of these items and asked Matthew whether he needed the valuation for probate or insurance purposes. For probate purposes, it is the value for which they could be sold which is needed; insurance value would be the cost of replacement, which is often considerably higher. The total value of Mrs Blake's jewellery came to £1,370, of which the diamond brooch was £250. Matthew had to pay a valuation fee, for which the jeweller gave him a receipt when he gave him the official valuation certificate. Matthew would include the valuation fee in the costs he would recover from the estate as executors' expenses in the administration account. If a valuable painting or piece of jewellery is disclosed, questions may arise about the origin of the item and when it was purchased. If earlier generations have not been completely honest, Matthew might receive an embarrassing questionnaire about the items.

The other item Matthew had to consider was the paintings. He had found, among the papers, the insurance policy for the home and contents and, with it, the latest endorsement for the renewal and review of the sum insured. In the contents section items above £300 had to be specifically mentioned. In that section, the paintings were specifically shown as £600, £500 and £400 respectively, which was considerably less than he had estimated, his mother-in-law having always told everyone how valuable they were. Matthew made a note of the values.

General valuation

More difficult to fix is a value for the great bulk of the household furniture and effects. How do you decide what the tables, chairs, beds, linen, cups and saucers, carpets, TV set, clothes and all the rest of it are actually worth? You have to decide what price they would get if sold to best advantage on the day of death. This means in practice what they would fetch at an auction. Of course, the second-hand value of the great majority of items is considerably less than the cost when new. For IHT, you do not consider the cost of replacement, but the price they would fetch if sold second-hand. The Capital Taxes Office (as it is still called) of the Inland Revenue does not expect you to provide an expert's valuation, or one that is accurate to within a few pounds, but a valuation that is honest and sensible, and says what the executor really thinks the items are worth.

This was Matthew's approach to the problem. He spent a Saturday afternoon going round the house with his brother-in-law Mark, assessing what was in the house. Where necessary, they discussed when, where and by whom various items had been bought, in order to exclude items which belonged to Mark already. Matthew made a few notes as they went along. A knowledgeable friend had a look at the carriage clock and put a value of £200 on it. In due course, he totted it all up. It came to more than his first guess. The figure he finally arrived at for the furniture and effects (excluding the pictures and jewellery which had been separately valued) was £1,645, plus £1,320 for the car.

One other article needed special consideration: the dishwasher. Matthew found that his mother-in-law was buying it on hire purchase, and there were four more payments of £11.55 each to be paid. How should this be dealt with in his valuation of Mrs Blake's property? Strictly speaking, the dishwasher itself was not something which belonged to Mrs Blake; it still belonged to the finance company. What she had owned – and which consequently had passed to the executors – was a right to become the owner of the dishwasher, when the remaining instalments had been paid, together with a right to use the dishwasher in the meantime. But it is not necessary to go through the solemn process of trying to value something so esoteric as a right of this kind. It is sufficient to take a common-sense attitude by valuing the article as if it had been part of what the deceased owned, along with everything else, and then to treat the instalments still to be paid as a debt due from her. This is what Matthew did about the dishwasher. His estimate of its current second-hand value, which he put at £90, was included as part of the £1,645, the value of the furniture and effects. The four outstanding hire purchase instalments of £11.55 each he would include as a debt of £46.20. He ignored the fact that these instalments were not actually due at the date of death, but only over the next four months. Matthew would have applied the same process of valuation if it had been the car, or any other articles, which Mrs Blake had been paying for on hire purchase. Where the figures are large, as for example on a car, it would be better to declare the net value as an asset after deducting the outstanding debt, rather than bringing this in as a separate debt.

Matthew now considered the simplest asset of them all: cash. In Mary Blake's handbag, in the drawer of her desk, and in one or two other places, Matthew found odd sums of cash: £18.40 in all.

Debts

If anyone had owed money to Mrs Blake, Matthew would have included it in the list of property declared for IHT. Any sums of money which are owed to the deceased count as assets. They are debts due to the estate. Items such as the dividend on the Stonehill Holdings shares, the pensions due to the date of death and any income tax repayment fall within this category.

Debts due from the deceased have to be listed, too. Any money which he owes reduces what he owns for the purpose of calculating his total property: the liabilities are deducted from the assets. These debts can consist of almost anything: fuel bills, tax, telephone account, amounts due on credit cards or credit accounts, hire purchase debts, an overdraft, for example. In addition, the funeral expenses (and the cost of a tombstone) are deducted.

Mrs Blake had a few debts. Matthew found an unpaid bill for gas, a telephone account, and the hire purchase for the dishwasher. In the course of the first few weeks after his mother-in-law's death, Matthew received two more bills, and these he added to the list: a bill for servicing the car, and another for some wines and spirits. Matthew assembled the invoices for these items, and wrote a short note to the companies and organisations who were owed money, explaining that they would be paid soon after probate was granted.

Not enough to meet the debts

Matthew had looked at all the assets and liabilities that he could find, and there were only very few debts and liabilities outstanding. In some cases, however, the debts can be a big problem in administering an estate. If you are involved in an estate where the deceased person had many debts and there is likely to be difficulty in being able to pay them, you should consult a solicitor.

Briefly, however, if the estate is insolvent (that is, there are insufficient assets to pay all the debts), the question is which of the various creditors obtains payment even though the deceased's property will not be sufficient to pay all the debts in full. Acts of Parliament lay down a special order. There are priorities for creditors who have their loans secured by a mortgage; funeral, testamentary and administrative expenses come next and have priority; then come VAT debts. It can thus happen that some creditors get paid in full and others get nothing. Or it can happen that all the creditors get at least something. In this case, an executor will often not take upon himself the administration of the estate but leave it for one or other of the creditors to take out a grant of letters of administration, as a creditor. There is little point in an executor getting involved where there will be no property actually to distribute to the beneficiaries.

If the estate is solvent (that is, there are sufficient assets to pay all the debts), the question is: which one(s) of all the various people entitled to the benefit of the deceased's estates will bear the debts? If there is any property which is mortgaged, then (unless the will specifies that the particular property should go to the recipient 'free from any mortgage debt outstanding against the property'), the building society or other creditor in whose favour the property is charged can ask for that property to be sold so that the loan can be repaid; or they might demand that the loan be paid by the beneficiary of that property. If such a property is part of the residuary estate and is not mentioned specifically in the will, the residuary beneficiary will be liable to pay the creditor who is secured by the property, if necessary by selling it.

Apart from this, the debts are usually paid out of the residuary estate. If there is not sufficient in the residuary estate, the money must come from that given as pecuniary legacies and the various pecuniary legacies to which the different people are entitled will be reduced proportionately until enough money has been raised to pay all the outstanding debts. If all the pecuniary legacies do not cover the debts, then any other property specifically given by the will must be utilised. Again, the various people entitled to these properties specifically given must bear the due proportion of the debts. If necessary, the properties concerned will have to be sold. There is no distinction between land, buildings, leases and any other moveable personal property in this respect.

If by this time all the debts have still not been paid, then the estate is insolvent. Seek professional legal advice.

Advertising for creditors

There is a special procedure for formally advertising for creditors in the *London Gazette* and in a newspaper for the area in which the deceased held property. The notice has to include the name of the person who has died, the date of death, and the name and address of the person to whom any creditors should submit their claim by a certain date – at least two months after the appearance of the advertisement.

Solicitors can put in this advertisement at any time, but the *London Gazette* will accept such a notice from ordinary personal representatives only after probate has been granted. But a local newspaper would accept an advertisement at any time.

Matthew did not consider that the situation in Mrs Blake's case would merit officially advertising for creditors, as there was no reason to suppose that she had any debts apart from those about which he already knew, or for which bills or accounts would come in within the next few weeks.

Applying for probate forms

Matthew knew that it would probably be a few weeks before all the information about valuing the estate would be complete and before he could proceed to the next stage: applying for the grant of probate. But it was not too soon to write for the forms that he would be needing for his application.

Matthew had received a booklet when he had registered the death, which contained the addresses of the District Registries of the Probate Registry, from which forms could be obtained. He wrote to the Probate Personal Application Department at the Principal Registry of the Family Division,* asking for the forms required to enable him to make a personal application for a grant of probate. (Had Mary Blake not left a will, he would have asked for those relevant to an application for a grant of letters of administration; the forms are the same.)

It is possible to write or telephone for the forms to a local District Probate Registry or Sub-Registry.

Finance for inheritance tax

Matthew next considered how to raise the money needed to pay the IHT. In his first rough calculation, he had estimated that the tax would be around £10,240. In the light of the way the valuation of the property was proceeding, it seemed likely that his first estimate had been too low. He could see that the estate would in fact come to about £250,000; the tax would be around £14,000.

In theory, the executors are faced with an odd dilemma. On the one hand, no bank or insurance company which holds money belonging to the estate is willing to hand any of it over to the executors until a grant of probate is obtained and produced to them; the probate is the only authority which can allow them to part with the money. On the other hand, the executors cannot obtain a grant of probate until they have actually paid the IHT, or at least most of it. How can they pay the tax, without being able to get their hands on the wherewithal to pay it?

From National Savings

If there are funds in the National Savings Bank (and funds cannot be made available from anywhere else), these can be used to pay the IHT; so can National Savings certificates, yearly-plan and premium bonds, also British savings bonds, and government stocks on the section of the National Savings Stock Register kept by National Savings, and money from save-as-you-earn contracts. A special system operates between the Personal Application Department of the Probate Registry and National Savings which enables this to be done. The executor has to explain when he first visits the Probate Registry that he needs to use the National Savings moneys for paying the tax; he will be given a note, on Probate Registry notepaper, showing that personal application has been made and stating the amount of inheritance tax and probate fees payable. The Probate Registry will then send this to the appropriate National Savings office, saying that the relevant savings bank account book, savings certificates, bond books, save-as-you-earn forms, or premium bonds, etc., had already been sent with form DNS 904, and quoting the reference number on the letter from National Savings, on which the executor had been told the value of the savings.

National Savings will then send a cheque for the tax and fees direct to the Probate Registry, and the balance of the National Savings moneys will be made available to the executors after probate is obtained. The balance of any save-as-you-earn or yearly-plan money that remains will then not earn any interest or enhancement prior to being repaid when the grant of probate is produced.

Other arrangements for IHT money

Generally, assets cannot be dealt with before there is a grant. But if the person who died had a building society account, it is possible that the society will release money from the account for the purpose of providing finance for IHT (and probate fees). A cheque will be issued not to the executors but made payable to the Inland Revenue for the IHT and to the Paymaster General for the probate fees.

If the person who died had a Girobank account, the executors may, subject to satisfactory identification, borrow for the purpose of paying IHT, so that a grant of probate may be obtained. The borrowing is limited to solvent estates and to the amount of the credit balance in the deceased's account.

Arrangements with the bank

Mrs Blake's building society was one of the smaller ones and did not have such an arrangement with the Inland Revenue (and, anyway, there might not have been enough in it for all the tax, plus the probate fees).

The obvious approach was to the bank where Mary Blake had kept her account, the Barminster Bank at Minford. The manager agreed to lend Matthew and Robert the money for paying the IHT. Banks usually do, unless the deceased had a sizeable overdraft when he died and the bank fears that it might not be met. In such a case, it can be useful if the executor can point out that there are, for example, share certificates of at least the value of the overdraft. The executor may be asked what shares will be sold and may have to agree that the actual sale will be carried out by the bank's broker and the overdraft paid off first, before the executor gets the rest of the proceeds.

Matthew did not have any difficulties in obtaining a loan limit of £25,000. This would easily cover all probate fees and tax, which seemed prudent to him. If you are not known to the bank involved you may experience some difficulty here.

It was arranged that an account (the 'executorship' account) should be opened at that branch in the name of the two executors. For the time being, the account was to be without funds, but Matthew would be sent a cheque book in the course of a few days. When the time came to pay the tax, Matthew and Robert would sign a cheque for the necessary amount, and the bank would meet it, although it could not be used for any other purpose until probate had been produced.

It was also arranged that a separate loan account should be opened which would fund the IHT and probate fees, specifically. The appropriate amounts would be transferred from the loan account to the executorship account to meet the cheques for IHT and probate fees. Where these items are kept identifiable from the amounts drawn on the executorship account, by prior arrangement with the bank, the interest payable is deductible from the income in the estate, for income tax purposes, for the first year of the period of administration in respect of IHT on personal moveable property. The Revenue sometimes allows a concession in respect of a loan for probate court fees too.

When, later on, the grant of probate had been obtained (but not before), the executors would be in a position to transfer the money in Mrs Blake's own account at the bank into the executorship account. This could then partly reduce the loan account balance, which would be completely paid off when the insurance moneys were received, the building society account closed, and some of the shares sold. In the meantime, the executors would have to pay interest on the whole amount outstanding, even though at the same branch there was another account, which was temporarily untouchable but which really belonged to the executors as well. Sometimes it is possible to arrange with the bank manager that, until probate is obtained, the two accounts shall be treated as one, so that the amount standing to the credit of the deceased's account may be set against the overdraft on the executorship account. But this cannot always be arranged, and there is no way of insisting that it should. Indeed, there is not even a way of insisting that the bank should provide an overdraft to pay the IHT.

It is often possible to arrange with the bank for the balance of an account at death to be placed on deposit in the deceased's name. The interest figure, which, in due course, would be added, would then have to be included in the income tax return for the administration period.

Finalising the valuation of the assets

It was not long before Matthew began to receive letters providing a precise valuation of the assets. He heard from the Department for National Savings about the savings bank account and the savings certificates; he heard from the insurance company that the policy money and the profits to be paid amounted to a total of £9,068.97.

The bank manager had handed a letter to Matthew when he went to discuss the IHT, and this letter stated the exact sum which stood to the credit of Mrs Blake's current account at the bank at the date of death: £193.52. The bank account was frozen as soon as the manager had been told of Mrs Blake's death. No further payment would be made out of the account either for cheques signed by Mrs Blake but not presented till after her death, or on banker's orders.

Matthew heard from the local inspector of taxes, who stated that a tax repayment would probably be due to his mother-in-law's estate, but required a tax form to be completed first. This did not worry Matthew because he knew that for the probate form he could put in an estimate of this figure, and notify the correct figure to the tax office at a later date.

Matthew heard from the building society about the mortgage on the house: the amount outstanding on the mortgage on 8 April 1997 was £25,124.35. He was also told the date of the mortgage, which he had not been able to find in Mrs Blake's records, but which he would need for the probate papers. The building society told him that they had received a letter from the Immortal Life Assurance Society that the proceeds due on the endowment life policy was £38,761.50. Interest would be payable on this sum until it was actually paid. The building society sent a claim form to be signed by the executors and also requested a death certificate to prove death upon which the endowment policy was payable. Matthew sent a copy of the death certificate back to the building society immediately. He would complete the claim form with Robert Blake as soon as probate had been granted. He would therefore expect to receive nearly £14,000 surplus from the life policy after repayment of the mortgage.

Then he heard from the secretary of the pension fund. There was £28.30 due for the proportion of Mrs Blake's pension for the part of the month of April during which she was alive. No other sum was due to the estate from the pension fund.

Matthew had also by now received all the letters from the company registrars, the Bank of England and the unit trust fund to whom he had written, and most of these confirmed the matters which he had asked. However, there was one unexpected letter, from the registrar of Coats Viyella plc. It read:

[Date]

Dear Sir,

Re: Mary Josephine Blake deceased

Thank you for your recent letter concerning the above-named deceased. I was sorry to hear of the death of our shareholder.

I confirm that there is a holding registered in the name of the deceased but the holding does not correlate exactly with the holding of which you advised us. The deceased is registered as the holder of 2,580 Coats Viyella plc Ordinary Shares. In 1988 there was a '1:5' bonus issue of shares and the certificate was sent out to the deceased on 31 July 1988 to her address at The Firs, Willow Lane, Minford, Surrey.

In case you are not able to locate the certificate, I enclose a form of statutory declaration indemnity and guarantee for completion in due course against which we will be prepared to issue a duplicate certificate so that the shares may then be dealt with. I must stress that a duplicate certificate will be issued only where you have made the fullest searches and the original certificate is not to be found, and also provided that you are able to complete the statutory declaration to the effect that you know of no sales or transfer of those shares by the deceased.

Please let me know if I can be of any further assistance to you.

Yours faithfully,

Registrar, Coats Viyella plc

This puzzled Matthew, because in the box with all the various deeds and documents for his mother-in-law, of Coats Viyella there were certificates totalling only 2,150 shares.

When a company does not want to distribute its dividend but wishes to retain the cash within the company, it will sometimes 'capitalise' the dividend and instead issue additional shares (called a bonus, or scrip, issue).

It seemed to Matthew that what had happened was that the certificate had been sent out to his mother-in-law, but that she had not placed it with the existing certificates. He would now have to search through all his mother-in-law's possessions once more to see if it could be found anywhere. He also discussed the matter with Robert and Mark; they did not know anything about this certificate either. They had another thorough search of all the possessions and papers in the house. It was nowhere to be found.

The next day, Matthew went to the bank and showed the letter from the registrar to the bank manager and asked if the bank would have a search to see if there were any documents and papers held for his mother-in-law. There were none. The immediate points were that the extra shares would have to be added to the value of the estate for the probate forms, and there would also be some additional inheritance tax payable. Matthew would have to add in a further 430 Coats Viyella plc ordinary shares at a value of 138p, increasing the total value of the shares by £593.40. They would now therefore total £75,686.98.

The question of the issuing of the duplicate certificate for the lost shares could be dealt with when probate had been granted.

A rights issue is when a company offers its shareholders further shares at less than the market price. If at the date of death payment for a rights issue is due, the registrar should be contacted immediately to see if he will agree to postpone payment until probate is received. If not, the funds would have to be raised elsewhere (from the bank or by a loan from the executors or beneficiaries to the estate), because the payment will secure a valuable asset to the estate. If payment is not made as required, the rights will be lost.

The same point could arise if a deceased had just acquired shares in a newly privatised company. Usually the original subscription will be for only part of the price, and the balance will be payable by the owner of the shares some months later. If the date is missed, the share can be forfeited or lost, so it is important to ensure that the money is available from some source; if necessary even before probate, if payment is required by a specific date. It is always wise to check the correct procedure with each company's registrar because practice can vary from company to company. Matthew saw that the British Gas and British Telecom shares were from recent privatisation issues but on checking the dates he realised that all payments had been made for these some time ago.

The building society had also replied telling him that the exact amount of capital held by his mother-in-law in the account was £16,727.48 and that there was a further £524.72 of interest accrued due at the date of death but not added to the account. The letter explained that interest was added on 20 June and 20 December each year, and that the December instalment had not yet been added to the book which was why the capital balance was for more than Matthew had expected.

Within a month of Mary Blake's death, Matthew had collected all the necessary information about the estate of his mother-in-law. The funeral account amounting to £1,200 was among the papers he collected together. Matthew was now able to complete the forms which would enable him to apply for a grant of probate.

Probate forms

Matthew had received the probate forms from the Personal Application Department of the Probate Registry in London, and it would be with that department at Somerset House in London that Matthew would be making all further arrangements. Had he lived outside London, he would have obtained the forms from, and would be making all further arrangements with, the nearest District Probate Registry or Sub-Registry. The procedure, after the forms are completed, can vary in minor respects not only between London and the provincial towns, but also between different District Registries.

In straightforward cases, there is a system which enables the matter to go through mainly by post and with only one visit to the Probate Registry. The executor has first of all to complete and send in the forms, so that they can be checked and the amounts of probate fees and IHT assessed; the registry officials prepare the document which the executor will then have to swear to be true. It is necessary for the executors to attend personally at the Probate Registry for this. If all is in order, an appointment is made, by post, for the executors to attend to swear the papers within about five weeks, but sometimes it takes considerably longer.

The time can also vary considerably between the different District Probate Registries. Some of the small local probate offices are sometimes manned only once a fortnight or even once a month. If you wish, you can find out from the registries in advance which is likely to be the quickest. But bear in mind that all the executors have to visit the registry in person at least once, and possibly more often, so you should choose one which is convenient for you.

Matthew and Robert both thought that London was most convenient for them.

Filling in probate forms

Read this section when you have the forms in front of you.

Matthew had received by post from the Probate Registry five forms that he would have to complete:

Form PA1: probate application form
Form PA5: matrimonial home questionnaire
Form IHT 205 (or IHT 44 if applicable): return of assets and debts
Form IHT 37: schedule of land and interests in land
Form IHT 40: schedule of stocks and shares.

Also in the package were three other items that he would refer to:

Form PA2: an explanation of making a personal application
Form PA3: a list of local probate offices
Form PA4: table of fees payable

Form PA1

To complete Form PA1 was quite simple. Only the white sections needed to be completed; the blue parts were for official use. First the form asked at which office the applicant wishes to attend. Matthew put London, Principal Registry. Then it asked for particulars about the deceased and some details of the will. Matthew had to complete particulars of the applicant (himself) and of any other applicants (his brother-in-law Robert). (The first named would be the one with whom the Personal Application Department of the Probate Registry would normally correspond, unless specially requested to do otherwise.)

The form has a space for naming any executors who are not applying for probate because they are dead, or do not wish to act as executor. If they do not wish to act but might apply to do so later, the probate office sends an official 'power reserved' letter which the non-acting executor has to sign. Even where a second executor does not want to act, it may be useful for him to sign this letter, just in case the first executor dies or becomes incapacitated before the grant of probate is obtained.

There is space for giving details of the surviving relatives which is particularly relevant where a will is not being proved by an executor.

Matthew found that he did not have to sign Form PA1. This was because the form is used by the Probate Registry as the basis for another form and an oath, which they prepare. These contain the same particulars, more or less, as Form PA1, but express them in the stipulated legal language and the oath is eventually sworn by the executors.

But the form had a reminder on it that with it would have to be sent the death certificate, the will and the completed form IHT 205. If this reveals that the estate exceeds the 'excepted estate' threshold, then form IHT 44 must be completed.

Form PA5

This form (or questionnaire) has to be completed if there is a widow(er) surviving the deceased and there is a matrimonial home which is in the sole name of the deceased. Because the property is in the name of the deceased only, the aim of the form is to ascertain whether the surviving widow(er) has any share or interest in the property in his or her own right, apart from any interest which he or she may receive under the will of the deceased. This can obviously affect the value of the deceased's estate and can be very important if the will does not provide for the property to pass to the surviving spouse. The executors would need to discuss this specifically with the deceased's widow(er).

The form itself is self-explanatory. It asks if the survivor wishes to claim any interest in the property even though the property was in the sole legal name of the deceased. The survivor might have acquired such an interest by providing part of the purchase money, or making financial contributions to the running of the house or even contributions physically towards the building or renovating or decoration of the property. All such matters should be declared on Form PA5.

There is a space for stating the percentage of the house's value which the surviving spouse claims to be entitled to. This might in due course have to be negotiated with the district valuer and also possibly with any other people who acquire the interest of the deceased in the property, if it does not all go to the surviving spouse in any event.

In the case of Matthew's mother-in-law the form did not apply: she was a widow herself and so there was no surviving spouse. Matthew wrote 'not applicable' on the form, and signed it as executor. Instead, he could have simply returned it blank.

Form IHT 205 and Form IHT 44

The rest of the forms were mainly concerned with providing details of the property which the deceased had left. **Form IHT 205** is a preliminary form, which is used by the Probate Registry to weed out those estates which are below the Inland Revenue threshold. If the gross estate comes to less than £180,000, there is no need for Form IHT 44 to be completed, but Form IHT 205 still has to be completed. This limit changes from time to time.

If the estate exceeds £180,000 or if you give certain answers on the IHT 205 form, you will have to complete Form IHT 44 instead of Form IHT 205.

There is space on **Form IHT 44** to fill in details of each of the assets which comprise the deceased's estate. The form contains reasonably clear instructions about what has to be included and how to fill it in.

Page 1 contains helpful notes; on pages 2 and 3 are various questions about gifts and trusts. On pages 4, 5 and 6 the assets including properties in and outside the United Kingdom have to be listed, and also debts due to the deceased, for example arrears of salary or pension payments. On page 7 all the debts owing by the deceased have to be listed.

Matthew left pages 2–4 for the time being (see page 136) and started filling in section 1 on page 5. **Item 1** in section 1 asked for details of Mary Blake's cash. Matthew had collected and counted this and it had come to £18.40 so that was the figure he entered. He had not considered it necessary to pay the actual notes and coins he had found belonging to his mother-in-law into the executorship bank account. It was quite in order to keep the cash to defray the small expenses of administration, but he made a note of everything he spent.

Item 2 was 'money at bank'. A separate note should be entered here for each bank account at any bank. For any deposit account, a note must be recorded of the interest accrued but not added to the account. The bank will supply these details in any particular case. For Matthew, there was just the 'current account at Barminster Bank, Minford'. This was what he entered on the form, and in the right-hand column '£193.52', the figure the bank had told him was the balance at the date of death.

Item 3 was for 'money at savings banks or in building, co-operative or friendly societies'. In Mrs Blake's case, there was the building society and the National Savings Bank. He therefore wrote as follows:

	£
National Savings Bank ordinary a/c with interest to date of death (exempt income tax)	389.20
Rockley Building Society Minford Branch	16,727.48
Interest to date of death accrued but not added	524.72
	£17,641.40

Matthew then wrote the total figure only (£17,641.40) in the right-hand column of Form IHT 44 opposite item 3.

Item 4 referred to 'household and personal goods'. Matthew had already carefully valued them. The value of the car was £1,320, the jewellery had been valued at £1,370, the pictures were £1,500, and £1,645 was the value of the remaining items. He put the figure of £5,835 in the 'gross value' column.

Item 5 related to National Savings investments and savings certificates. Here Matthew wrote 'see letter': he would attach to Form IHT 44 the letter from National Savings showing the value of the savings certificates. The figure he wrote in the right-hand column was £742.50. He kept a note of the reference number on the letter from National Savings as he would need to quote it when it came to cashing the savings certificates after probate had been obtained.

Item 6 was for premium bonds. These are worth their face value so Matthew filled in £1,500 in the right-hand column.

Item 7 on the form said 'Stocks, shares or investments quoted on the Stock Exchange including unit trusts'. Even if Mrs Blake had owned only one or two lots of shares, Matthew should just give the total here, using Form IHT 40 for the individual details. He put Form IHT 44 on one side for the moment.

Form IHT 40

Form IHT 40 is buff-coloured and ruled into columns to enable the necessary data about the stocks and shares to be set out in tabular form. When completed, Form IHT 40 looked rather like the valuation which Matthew had prepared for his own benefit, but rearranged in the order in which they appear in the official list.

The form was headed 'Schedule of stocks and shares'. In **column 1** it was necessary to specify the type of stock or shares, the name of the company and also the unit of quotation. This means the unit of the stock or shares, the value of which was quoted on the Stock Exchange. In the case of stock, the unit of quotation is often £1, but not necessarily so. In the case of shares, the unit of quotation is one share, as a rule. The exact type of denomination of stock and shares can be found simply by looking at the certificates. If the shares are 'bearer' shares, it means that they are owned by whoever has the rightful possession of the certificate, and the names of the owner will not appear. For the unit trusts in Mrs Blake's holdings, Matthew simply put 'Units' as the unit of quotation.

Column 2 in Form IHT 40 asked for the quantity which the deceased had held of the investment concerned, in terms of so much of the unit of quotation, referred to in the previous column.

Column 3 asked for the market price at date of valuation, which means the date of death or the date nearest to it for which the *Stock Exchange Daily Official List* was published. This is where the formula of 'one quarter up' applies. Having found the quotations in the *Stock Exchange Daily Official List*, Matthew entered on the form the figure one quarter up from the lower price. This was the recognised market value for the purpose of assessing inheritance tax.

Column 4 to be completed on Form IHT 40 asked for the principal value at date of valuation. Matthew arrived at this by multiplying the number of shares or the amount of stock by the market price at date of death.

Matthew completed Form IHT 40 with particulars of the ten holdings of stocks and shares that Mary Blake had owned, listing 2,580 Coats Viyella shares to include those covered by the lost certificate. The total value of these was £3,560.40 instead of £2,967 which he had previously recorded. All the others were the same, including the Allied Dunbar Unit Trust. (By the price for the Stonehill Holdings shares, Matthew put 'xd', indicating that the price was quoted ex-dividend on the day concerned; the amount of the dividend declared, yet to be received, would have to be included later on in the form.) The total value came to £75,686.98.

Back to Form IHT 44

He wrote the words 'see Form IHT 40' alongside item 7 to indicate where full details could be found of how the £75,686.98 was made up, and also wrote this figure in the column alongside.

Item 8 This section he left blank. If there had been holdings in private companies (these are relatively rare) he might have been wise to seek legal advice.

Item 9, on page 6, was for insurance policies. **Part (a)** related to policies on Mrs Blake's life. Where the form asked for the name of the company, Matthew filled in 'Bridstow Insurance Company' and the amount to be shown in the figures column was the amount to be paid in respect of the policy including bonuses. The letter from the insurance company had stated this amount: £9,068.97. Matthew also had to add in this section the endowment policy from the Immortal Life Assurance Society, even though this would be used to pay off the mortgage. He put

'Immortal Life Assurance Society endowment policy – £38,761.50'.

Part (b) of Item 9 concerned policies taken out by the deceased on someone else's life, someone who was still alive. A woman may take out a policy on the life of her husband, for instance, because she has a vital financial interest in his continued ability to earn money; an employer may insure the life of a crucial employee, or one partner in a business take out a policy on the life of another partner. Where this happens, the policy counts as an asset in the estate of the person who took out the policy, and the value to be shown is the surrender value at the date of death (which the insurance company would give in a letter to the executors). Mrs Blake had no such policies so Matthew wrote 'none' in the right-hand column. He left this section blank. Had there been such a policy the insurance company would have informed him of its value when he notified them of the death.

It can sometimes happen that there is a policy stated to be written under the 'Married Women's Property Act'. This usually applies where the policy is taken out on the life of a husband but has been assigned to the wife so that on the death of the husband the wife will receive the moneys automatically on proof of death and regardless of the grant of probate. It does not have to be declared on the Form IHT 44 because the proceeds do not belong to the deceased's estate, but to the widow.

Item 10 asked for 'amounts which employers owe'. The first part deals with any amounts due from the employer if the deceased was working at the time of his death, for example any amount of wages still owed, or commissions not yet received.

No amount was owed in Mary Blake's case and this is what Matthew wrote on the form. However, the second part of the question asked for details of any other benefits due to the deceased and this would include such things as employer's pension payments. Under her husband's pension scheme, Mary Blake, as his widow, was entitled to receive a pension for the rest of her life.

The proportion of Mrs Blake's pension from her late husband's former employer's pension fund up to the date of her death amounted to £28.30. Matthew entered this amount on the form.

Item 11 asked for details of 'reversion'. Reversions are interests in trust property, often under the will of someone who might have died many years ago, which are not payable until the death of some other person. These are not taxable as part of a deceased's estate but they still have to be declared. Mrs Blake's estate had no such interest so Matthew again entered 'none'. If Mrs Blake had been left some money or property in the will of somebody who had died before her but the precise amount was not yet known, Matthew would have written to the executors to find out an approximate amount and would have notified the Capital Taxes Office of the correct amount in due course.

Item 13 covered a civil servant's death benefit, the capital sum paid to the estate of permanent civil servants if they die in service. Mary Blake had not been a civil servant, so there was 'none' to fill in there.

Item 14, 'other assets', was an omnibus item, the place to fill in details of almost anything not covered elsewhere. Matthew included here the arrears of the state retirement pension, amounting to £41.07. He completed this part of the form with these bare details, and did not add any particulars, or include supporting evidence. The other item was the dividend on the shares quoted 'ex-dividend'. What Matthew wrote here was 'Dividend declared at the date of death 1.715p per share on 15,000 shares in Stonehill Holdings plc – see Form IHT 40' and he filled in a figure for this item of £205.80 (£257.25 less 20% for income tax). He would be receiving a dividend warrant for the amount shortly. He had told the company of Mary Blake's death, so the warrant would be made out to Mary Blake's executors, after probate had been obtained.

Item 15 applies only where the deceased owned a business; Mary Blake did not, and Matthew put 'none' against the item.

Item 16 was the one for the house. It asked about 'Freehold and leasehold property'. Matthew completed the address of the house which Mrs Blake had owned and lived in: The Firs, Willow Lane, Minford. Alongside, he wrote his estimate of the value of the house: £125,000. If the property was co-owned with someone else as tenants-in-common the value of the deceased's share should be entered here, but not if it was owned as joint tenants. At this point, he again put Form IHT 44 on one side.

Form IHT 37

The form was headed 'Schedule of land and interests in land'. It was designed to cover a great variety of properties, not only houses. **Column 2** asked for a description of the property, and Matthew wrote its postal address including postcode. **Column 3** asked for details of tenure; the answer was 'freehold'. If the property was a flat then it will almost certainly be 'leasehold' and with the deeds of the property there will be a lease, maybe 20–30 pages long, as well as a title certificate.

Column 4 applied to any property that was let on a landlord and tenant basis; Matthew left it blank.

Column 5 covered agricultural land; Matthew left it blank.

The important question came in **column 6**: the gross value. This meant the capital value on the open market at the date of death. This was where Matthew filled in the figure £125,000. The outstanding amount of the mortgage debt is treated separately as a debt for IHT purposes, rather than an amount by which the value of the property is reduced. Only property which has a capital value has to be included for IHT. A tenancy of a house or flat normally has no capital value and nothing need be said about it in the probate forms. A tenancy is an arrangement in which a full rent is paid regularly. In a long leasehold, there is no rent, or a small ground rent may be payable. Such a leasehold has a capital value and should be included here.

In the 'notes' on the form, there were questions about sales or any proposed sale of any of the property. Matthew did not have anything to say in reply.

If a spouse is claiming any share in a property which was in the sole name of the deceased wife or husband, the full value should be entered on this form, and also on Form IHT 44. But if 'see Form PA5' is written against the figure, the Probate Registry (in consultation with the Inland Revenue) may amend the value.

At the top of the form, Matthew wrote Mrs Blake's name against 'Deceased or Transferor', and the date of her death, and in the appropriate box his own name and address as the person to whom the valuation office should send any communication. The 'CTO Reference' he left blank: that would be allocated by the Inland Revenue.

Back to Form IHT 44 again

Page 7 was for recording all the debts and liabilities of the estate. **Item 17** was for details of the funeral expenses. Matthew had received the undertaker's account, so he inserted their details and the figure £1,200 in the right-hand column.

Item 18 was for other debts due to UK residents. Matthew had earlier assembled the bills which he had been able to find, for gas, telephone, wines and spirits, car service and hire purchase on the dishwasher. Matthew filled in to whom money was owed: description – gas, telephone, etc. – and in the right-hand column the amount of each debt. The debts in this section totalled £227.06.

Item 19 was for mortgages due to UK residents. This applied in Mary Blake's case, and Matthew filled in the details as requested – the amount outstanding at the date of death, £25,124.35, and the date of the mortgage which the building society had told him. He gave the address of the property and details of the building society. If the property had been jointly owned, only the deceased's share of the mortgage (one half where the property is held as joint tenants) should be entered.

Sometimes there is a life insurance policy, or mortgage protection policy, in conjunction with a mortgage which will pay out on the death of the owner (and if the policy is payable to the estate, it is counted in for IHT purposes). There is a space for recording this below the mortgage details. Matthew therefore entered the following: 'Immortal Life Assurance Society endowment mortgage life assurance policy proceeds payable to mortgagee.' (He had already recorded the details of the policy as directed on page 6 item 9 of the form.)

Section 2 on page 7 of Form IHT 44 asked for details of all assets outside the UK in the deceased's sole name (not joint assets). This can include shares in foreign companies, villas in Spain, or a business carried on abroad. All debts due to anyone resident outside the United Kingdom can be included here. There were none in Mary Blake's estate so Matthew left these blank.

The earlier part of the form (on pages 2 and 3) asked a number of questions about the estate, and Mrs Blake's affairs generally, which could have a bearing on the amount of tax payable.

Question 1 on page 2 concerned assets nominated by the deceased during his lifetime in favour of any person. These do not form part of the deceased's estate, and so do not pass through the hands of the personal representatives, but pass direct to the person to whom they are nominated. Nevertheless, they have to be declared for the purposes of IHT, and details must be included. There being none in Mary Blake's case, Matthew ticked No.

Question 2 was about gifts and other transfers made by Mrs Blake before her death. In order to calculate the tax payable on death, the Capital Taxes Office needs to have full information about all relevant gifts with which the deceased was concerned because this will affect the point on the inheritance tax scale at which the rates commence (as explained on page 17).

On the form, details of all gifts, the date, value, to whom given and address have to be stated. But there are some exceptions, listed on page 2: gifts between husband and wife and wedding presents do not usually count, and you can ignore Christmas presents and birthday presents within the stated limits. Also gifts in any one year under £3,000 are exempt and need not be listed (the figure for exempt gifts is lower for earlier years). Also, where a person has established a pattern of making gifts out of his excess income without affecting his standard of living, these are exempt.

Question 2 also refers to gifts and transfers made within seven years of the date of death. For these purposes, a settlement is a gift which is not to one person absolutely, but one where the property has to be held on trust for the benefit of others. Usually the answer is 'no', as was the case for Mrs Blake. Nor had Mary Blake paid the premium on any life insurance policy for the benefit of anyone else; so Matthew ticked 'No' to that part of the question.

(See below under Question 4 for more light on Question 2b.)

Item d within question 2 related to any other transfer of value. The phrase 'transfer of value' means any transaction where there is some element of gift, in other words the transfer or even sale of any property for less than the full market value, subject to the exemptions set out. Matthew did not know of any, so he ticked the 'No' box. If there is any doubt, an executor or intending administrator has a positive duty to make all diligent enquiries. If you sold some property even at full market value but to a relative, this must be declared.

If there had been any large gift in Mary Blake's life in respect of which she had been obliged to fill in a tax return at that time (to assess any lifetime tax payable), the full reference of that return has to be given so that the Inland Revenue can trace the record through it.

Question 3 on page 3 about gifts with reservation asked if the deceased created a trust but reserved an interest. This would include a gift of a house where the deceased reserved the right to remain living in it after making the gift. The answer was 'no'.

Question 4 on page 3 was about assets held in trust. This is an arrangement whereby a person transfers some of his property (generally some investments) during his lifetime to trustees who are directed to pay the income from the investments to one person for a period, often for that person's life, and then to divide up the capital among others. Wealthy people often used to make a trust on the marriage of one of their children, when it was called a marriage settlement. A similar sort of disposition of any property can also be made in a person's will, but then it operates only after the death of the person who makes it. Mrs Blake had not been entitled to an interest under a settlement during her lifetime. Matthew therefore put a tick in the 'No' box.

The distinction between this question and the trusts in question 2b above on page 2 is that here they are asking about all trusts in which Mary Blake was entitled to any interest, for example if she was receiving the income from a settlement or trust which someone else had made for her benefit. The trusts referred to in question 2b are those which she made, if any, for the benefit of other people. If there are any, you should consult a solicitor.

Question 5 on page 3 of Form IHT 44 asked whether any sum of money or annuity became payable on the death to any person under a superannuation scheme. In Mary Blake's case the answer to this was 'No'. Where, under an occupational pensions scheme, a lump sum or a pension now becomes payable to a widow, the executors should attach a copy of the letter from the secretary of the staff pension scheme concerned.

Regardless of whether there will be any IHT payable, the Inland Revenue requires details of all property owned by the deceased, including any jointly held (even if the co-owner is the deceased's spouse and therefore exempt from IHT).

Question 6B on page 4 was for ascertaining the extent of the deceased's share in any land or buildings owned jointly with other people. Who contributed what proportion of the purchase money will, to a great extent, govern the shares in the ownership at the time of death. But if the only co-owners are husband and wife, the property is usually deemed to be equally owned. The form asks about the value of the deceased's share. If the property is held as tenants-in-common (rather than joint tenants) by two people other than husband and wife, it is usually possible to argue that the value is somewhat reduced, perhaps 15 per cent less than the proportion of the open market value of the property with vacant possession. The value declared for **question 6B, part 4** on page 4 should take account of this.

Part 5 of section 6B asks whether the share accrued by survivorship (that is, as joint tenants), or if it passed by will or intestacy (owned as tenants-in-common). If it is owned as tenants-in-common, it has to be included in paragraph 15 (or section 2 if outside the UK).

Question 6A on page 4 deals with other jointly owned property. The principles are largely the same as in (6B). Again, between husband and wife it is usually assumed that the property is equally owned. In other cases, calculations of all the contributions and withdrawals by each of the owners may have to be made, unless it can be shown that there was an intention that the property was to be owned equally.

For Matthew, completing this page was easy. There was no jointly held property in Mary Blake's case, so Matthew simply ticked the 'No' box.

Form IHT 44 contains boxes for totalling up the various parts of the estate. From the figures on the form, Matthew worked out what the net estate would come to, because probate fee and inheritance tax would be based on this. The figure he arrived at was £248,172.03.

Sending off the forms

Matthew arranged a meeting with Robert, his brother-in-law and co-executor, and went carefully through the completed forms with him, explaining each item to him to be sure he understood it and that it was accurately completed. Of the forms which Matthew had completed, only Forms IHT 44 and IHT 205 needed to be signed.

Matthew would be posting the original of Mrs Blake's will to the Probate Registry. Then, having taken a photocopy of everything, he bundled into the large envelope, which had come with the forms, these documents: the will, death certificate, Form IHT 44, Form IHT 37, Form IHT 40 and Form PA5. To Form IHT 44 he attached the original letter from National Savings about the savings certificates and the piece of paper with 'Schedule A'. It is important that none of the forms or letters is clipped or pinned to the will.

Matthew sent the envelope, by recorded delivery, to the Personal Application Department of the Probate Registry* in London. A few weeks later he received a form from the registry, which asked him and Robert Blake to come to Somerset House, at a stated time on a particular day, 10.30 a.m. on 30 June 1997.

He would be sure to take his file of background papers and the fee.

Fees

The probate fees are charges made by the Probate Registry for dealing with the papers and issuing the grant of probate. They are calculated on the amount of the net estate, as declared for the purpose of inheritance tax (excluding any part of the estate passing by survivorship).

Form PA4 gives a list of the fees, as a guide: it would be wise to confirm the actual amount payable before you attend the interview at the Probate Registry.

The probate fees must be paid when the personal representatives go to the Registry to swear the papers. Payment can be made by cheque, banker's draft, postal order or in cash. In Mary

Blake's case, with a net estate of £248,172.03, the total fees would come to £599, made up as follows: £300 for the first £200,000, plus £50 for the next £48,172.03 in respect of the court fee, and an additional £249 representing £1 for every £1,000 of the net estate in respect of the personal application fee.

Matthew would draw a cheque for £601.50 made payable to HM Paymaster General, on the executorship account, which he and Robert had recently opened at the bank. The extra £2.50, on top of the £599 probate fees, was for ten official copies of the probate, at 25p each. Matthew had already arranged with the bank manager for the temporary overdraft.

At the Probate Registry

On the day appointed for their interview at the Probate Registry, Robert Blake and Matthew went to Somerset House in The Strand, near the Aldwych and King's College, London. (You can go to the Probate Registry that is most convenient to you.) Matthew took with him to the Probate Registry the file with all the papers he had accumulated in connection with Mrs Blake's estate so that he could check the accuracy of the forms they would be asked to swear as being correct. They made their way to the Personal Application Department as directed, and handed in the form they had been sent. A few minutes later they were asked to the room of the commissioner who would deal with their case.

The information which Matthew had supplied on the various probate forms had been translated on to formal printed legal documents, the executor's oath and Inland Revenue account. In the blanks were various details of the life, death and family of Mary Josephine Blake and her property. The commissioner explained that before signing they ought to be completely satisfied that the details in the forms were true in every respect. As personal representatives, theirs was the responsibility that everything was completely and accurately stated. Robert and Matthew carefully went through each part of the oath and account which seemed to tally exactly with the information which Matthew had supplied.

Satisfied that everything was in order, both Matthew and Robert signed the oath in the space provided at the end. They also signed the original will, as indicated to them by the commissioner; the oath contained a clause identifying the will as Mary Blake's. Then, at the request of the commissioner, each of them stood up in turn, held up a copy of the New Testament in the right hand and repeated aloud these words after the commissioner: 'I swear by almighty God that this is my name and handwriting, and that the contents of this my oath are true and that this is the will referred to.' As each said the words '... name and handwriting' the commissioner pointed to their signatures on the oath, and likewise with the will.

Instead of swearing on the Bible (New Testament or Old Testament), a personal representative who has grounds for objecting to taking an oath can affirm by holding up his right hand and saying: 'I solemnly and sincerely affirm that this ...'

The commissioner signed beneath each of their signatures and signed the will below where they had signed it. Their business at the Probate Registry was now done, except for paying the probate fees. Matthew produced the cheque to the cashier, who checked it with the form and the records. Matthew also ordered ten 'sealed' copies of the grant of probate, when it was issued. He reckoned that he would need this number of copies to send out, in order to avoid delays in completing the administration of the estate. These official copies are not ordinary photocopies (which anyone could take) but are copies which bear the impress of the court's seal and this is what shows them as authoritative.

Letters of administration

If Mrs Blake had left no will, her next of kin – her children, or one of them – would have been applying for a grant of letters of administration, instead of probate; the same would have been the case if she had left a will but it had appointed no executors, or if the executors appointed in the will did not apply for probate. In those cases, the grant would be called 'letters of administration with the will annexed'.

When letters of administration are being sought, the administrators may in some cases have to provide a guarantee. This is likely to happen only where the beneficiaries are under age or mentally disabled. The guarantee is provided by an insurance company or by individuals who undertake to make good – up to the gross value of the estate – any deficiency caused by the administrators failing in their duties. It is more likely to be required when an administrator is out of the country.

An insurance company will charge a fee for agreeing to act as guarantor, and will usually have the forms already drawn up.

Letters of administration may also be taken out by creditors of an estate if executors will not apply for probate – for example, if there are insufficient assets to pay all the creditors and legatees.

Inheritance tax

IHT, on most assets, has to be paid before the grant of probate is issued. That is why it is often necessary to borrow money to pay the tax: in a sense, it has to be paid in advance, that is, before the assets of the estate can be made available for the purpose of paying the tax. Interest is charged on all outstanding IHT from the end of the sixth month after death, at 4% per annum.

But for farm land, a family business and some unquoted shares, it is possible to pay IHT by instalments in 10 yearly payments. (The whole of the outstanding tax becomes immediately due if the property is sold.)

It is worth considering taking up the instalments option where this is allowed. This can operate as a means of delaying the payment of most of the tax on the property until after you have got the grant of probate, so saving having to pay interest on a loan or overdraft, which is generally at a higher rate than that charged on overdue tax.

Matthew received a form from the probate office, headed 'The estate of *Mary Josephine Blake* deceased' and informing him that in addition to the probate fees which he had already paid he should now send a cheque for IHT, made payable to 'Inland Revenue', for £13,268.81. The assessment of IHT was the official calculation of tax on the basis of the value of the net estate, as disclosed in the forms they had completed. The net estate means the value of the assets, less the debts (including the mortgage) and the funeral expenses.

IHT on death is charged as follows. All property left to the widow or widower is exempt from inheritance tax. The first £215,000 of the net estate is also exempt from tax; that is, on the estate not left to the widow or widower, you pay only on the excess over £215,000. After these exemptions, IHT is payable at 40% on the rest of the net estate.

Tax on the estate of Mrs Blake (£248,172.03 net) was calculated as follows:

on the slice to £215,000.00 at nil	=	nil
on the slice £215,000.00 to £248,172.03 at 40%	=	£13,268.81
total tax payable	=	£13,268.81

Matthew could have made arrangements with the building society to pay the IHT and probate fees direct from the building society account, but having made arrangements with the bank he decided to stick with them.

He noted that he had not quite finished with IHT: it would have to be adjusted later (see page 150).

The grant

While there may be an interval of six weeks or more between lodging the probate papers and being asked to come to the registry to sign and swear them, after that things tend to move quickly. If there is no IHT to be paid, for instance where the net estate is less than £215,000 or where all the deceased's property goes to the spouse, the grant of probate (or letters of administration) will be issued within a few days.

If IHT has to be paid, it takes two or three weeks from when the papers are signed and sworn to being told how much IHT is payable, and the grant is usually ready within a week of the IHT cheque being cleared. If there is likely to be any delay, or a technicality is holding things up, the personal representatives should be informed by the Probate Registry. A further visit to the registry is sometimes necessary.

In Matthew's case, there was no hitch: the grant of probate arrived by first-class post a few weeks later.

It was signed by an officer of the Probate Registry, and the essence of it read as follows: '... the last Will and Testament (a copy of which is hereunto annexed) of the said deceased was proved and registered in the Principal Probate Registry of the

High Court of Justice and administration of all the estate which by law devolves to and vests in the personal representative of the said deceased was granted by the aforesaid court to Matthew John Seaton and Robert Anthony Blake.'

Any property which passes by survivorship does not 'devolve to' the personal representatives but goes automatically to the survivor. (This is why it is excluded from the calculation of probate fees even though not excluded from calculations for inheritance tax, where applicable.)

At the end of the document, it stated the gross and net estates (i.e. before and after deduction of debts) but the amount of tax was not disclosed. The press often publish in the newspapers the value of the estates of famous people who have died. It is seldom a true indication of their wealth because it takes no account of any jointly owned property, or any trusts to which they are entitled, nor, for that matter, of the inheritance tax to be paid out which will reduce the estate.

Attached to the grant of probate was a photocopy of the will, the original will being kept at Somerset House in London; Matthew noticed that each page of the copy will bore the impress of the court's official seal. It was accompanied by a note which very briefly explained the procedure for collecting in the estate and advised representatives to obtain legal advice in the event of any dispute or difficulty.

The grant was what they had been striving for. It confirmed that they were entitled to deal with Mrs Blake's property, to pay her debts, and then to distribute the property in accordance with her will. It is a public document in the sense that anybody, including any beneficiary, and even the press, can obtain a copy of it or of the will from Somerset House for a small fee. Copies of the will or the grant can also be obtained at the Probate Registry where they were issued.

Sometimes there is no apparent need to obtain a grant of probate or letters of administration if the estate is very straightforward because, for example, all the property is jointly owned, there is no tax to be paid or there are no assets which require a grant of probate to be produced.

However, it can happen that, subsequently, some other asset comes to light (for example, a share certificate) or money becomes payable to the deceased's estate as a result of the death of some other person many years later. In such a case, the assets can be paid over or transferred to the deceased's estate only on production of a grant of probate or letters of administration to ensure that the assets will be paid over to the correct person. In that case, a grant of probate would need to be obtained. There is no difference in the procedures for obtaining it and no time limit (although in practice the lapse of time can make it more difficult to locate and trace what assets and liabilities there were at the date of death). Inheritance tax, or capital transfer tax, or even estate duty, may be payable and will be assessed as at the date of the death of the deceased for whom probate is being sought (but probate fees are assessed as at the time when the papers are lodged for probate). If tax becomes payable, then interest may be charged on the amount due because of the time which has elapsed since the date of death.

Administration

When he had the probate, Matthew lost no time in proceeding with the administration. Enclosed with the probate were the ten sealed copies of it for which he had asked. With these, it was possible to proceed with the administration more quickly. Instead of having to send the probate in turn to each organisation requiring to see it, it was possible to send it to the bank, the insurance company, National Savings and the inspector of taxes (who would require the original probate with the attached copy will), for instance, and some of the companies in which Mary Blake had investments, all on the same day, by sending one of the sealed copies to each of them.

Matthew wrote a similar letter to all those who had to see the probate: the insurance company, the secretary of the firm's pension scheme, the Department of Social Security (about the arrears of retirement pension) and the inspector of taxes (about the tax refund).

[Date]

Dear Sir,

Re: Mary Josephine Blake deceased

I enclose a sealed copy of the probate of the will of the above for

registration with you. Please return it to me when this has been done, and send me what is due to the estate as described in your letter to me of ...
Yours faithfully,

He had previously received payment application forms for the various National Savings assets, when he asked for their valuations. He now completed and signed these forms, as executor, and returned them to National Savings with a sealed copy of the grant of probate.

To the bank manager, Matthew wrote the following letter:

[Date]

Dear Sir,

Re: Mary Josephine Blake deceased

I now enclose a sealed copy of the probate of the will and shall be glad if you will return it to me when you have recorded details of it. Will you please now close the deceased's current account at your branch and transfer the money in it to the executorship account which my co-executor (Robert A. Blake) and I recently opened at your branch.

I am now collecting the rest of the assets and this will result in our being able to pay off the loan account in the near future.

Yours faithfully,

There was £193.52 in Mary Blake's current account when she died. The cheques for the IHT (£13,268.81) and the probate fees (£601.50) had given rise to a debit amounting to £13,870.31 on the loan account and this was now slightly reduced by the funds from the deceased's own bank account. Banks as a rule do not allow the credit on the deceased's bank account to be treated as available for a beneficiary's use until probate is obtained. As a result a son, for instance, may be faced with paying overdraft interest to a bank even though there is money available in the same bank which will eventually be his when probate has been granted.

Within a few days, the £9,068.97 from the insurance company arrived and, not long after, the money from National Savings, including the £1,500 from the premium bonds. No premium bond prizes had been declared in the interim. Premium bonds are not transferable and must be repaid, but the other National Savings products do not have to be encashed but can be simply transferred to beneficiaries after probate. On some types of National Savings there is a limit to the total amount any one person is allowed to hold, but this limit can be exceeded if the excess is the result of transferring to the inheritor the savings held by the deceased. Matthew also received the closing balance in the National Savings Bank ordinary account of £391.14, which included the small amount of income for the period from the date of death (£1.94). This was exempt from income tax.

When a copy of the probate was returned by one of the organisations that owed money to the estate, Matthew sent it off to any others who had not yet seen it. All who had to pay money to the executors required to see it, and enter details of it in their records; this is often referred to as 'registering the probate'. They usually put their stamp on the back of the probate.

Soon all the money which was to be paid to the estate had been received by Matthew and paid into the executorship account at the bank. Matthew kept a note of all of these:

	£
National Savings Bank account	391.14
Life insurance	9,068.97
Premium bonds	1,500.00
Building society account	17,863.14
Savings certificates	742.50
Pension from employers	28.30
Pension from state	41.07
Dividend payable on Stonehill Holdings plc shares	205.80
Total amounts received	£29,840.92

The building society figure was for more than the amount declared at the date of death because of the additional interest to the date of closing the account.

Matthew realised that there was still £13,870.31 outstanding on the loan account, so he wrote to the bank stating that all these amounts had been paid into the executors' account and could the bank now please transfer sufficient to repay the loan account, together with all interest due, up to the date of closing the account? He asked the bank to send him a note of the interest on that account to the date of closing, so that this could be deducted later on from any income tax assessed on the estate.

He received a reply from the bank that the interest to the closing of the executors' loan account was £235.14, so that after all the amounts had been credited, the executor's account had a total of £15,928.99.

Finding unknown creditors

If a personal representative has reason to wonder whether all the deceased's debts have come to his notice, there is a special procedure, which involves advertising for creditors. After probate, the personal representative puts an advertisement in the *London Gazette* and a local newspaper announcing that all claims against the estate have to be made by a date not less than two months ahead. There is a standard way of setting out the notice. Where this is done in the official way, the personal representative will then be quite safe in dealing with the estate on the basis of the debts known to him on the date by which claims have to be made, according to the advertisements.

If a personal representative does not advertise for creditors in this way, there is always a danger, however slight, that after he has parted with the assets to the beneficiaries, some unknown creditor appears on the scene and justifiably claims that the deceased owed him money. If that were to happen, the personal representative would have to pay the debt out of his own pocket.

The lost share certificate

Now that probate had been granted, Matthew could deal with the question of the lost share certificate for 430 shares in Coats Viyella plc. Each company registrar may have a different procedure to replace a lost certificate. Matthew looked out the forms which the registrar of Coats Viyella had sent to him. There was a statutory declaration which he and Robert had to sign to the effect that they had made all due searches and had not found the certificate and that they believed it to be lost and that, so far as they were aware, Mrs Blake had not sold or signed any form of transfer of those shares.

There was another form which they were required to sign: an indemnity to the company against any loss which might be suffered if the certificate should later turn up in the hands of some rightful owner. The registrar would be prepared to issue the duplicate certificate only if Matthew and Robert signed this form of indemnity. On the same form, there was a section for a bank to guarantee the indemnity so that the loss would not fall on Matthew and Robert at some time in the future. Matthew discussed this matter with the bank manager at the Barminster Bank and the bank agreed to countersign the form of guarantee for a fee of £25 which would be deducted from the executors' account. To complete the statutory declaration, Matthew and Robert had to swear it before a solicitor. Any solicitor will be prepared to do this but will charge £5 each for this service.

There was no need for Robert to come to London to attend to this one item; it was not necessary for them both to sign in the same place or at the same time, so Matthew sent the form to Robert. Within a few days he received the declaration back from Robert and went to find a solicitor in the High Street at Minford. It is quite acceptable to walk into any solicitor's office even if you have had no previous dealings with the firm. Matthew and Robert each made a note of the £5 cash which they had paid out to the solicitors because this was a proper cost of the administration of the estate to be reclaimed.

Matthew then wrote to the registrar of Coats Viyella plc, enclosing the sealed copy probate, the statutory declaration indemnity, guarantee and the share certificates for the 2,150 shares. By 1 August he had received back the new share certificate showing the names of himself and Robert, the executors of Mary Josephine Blake, as the registered owners of 2,580 Coats Viyella shares.

He would leave the rest of the shares to be dealt with later when he knew which were going to be sold and which were going to be retained and distributed to the beneficiaries.

IHT rectification

When there is no provisional agreement with the district valuer about the value of a house, the first contact with him is after probate has been obtained. Where this happens, the value of the house as finally agreed with the district valuer may be higher than the value included in the Inland Revenue account. This results in a further payment of IHT having to be made at this stage.

Matthew heard from the district valuer for Minford who considered that Matthew's figure of £125,000 for The Firs was too low. After some bargaining, they agreed that the figure should be £127,500, so that a further £1,000 of tax (for the extra £2,500 at 40%) would be due. In fact, Matthew had not yet received a further assessment from the Inland Revenue but would have to pay when he did.

Additional tax would also become due if the executors discovered some asset of which they had had no knowledge when the papers were signed. They might, for instance, find that the deceased had had a deposit account at a bank which was different from the bank where he kept his current account, or an 'ex-dividend' amount had not been ascertainable in time. Where this happens, details have to be given to the capital taxes office, and it may be necessary to sign a further, corrective, document. Occasionally, if an asset was mistakenly overestimated in value, or if a new debt appears, there may be some inheritance tax to be returned to the personal representatives.

Having sent a tax return and the original probate of the will to the inspector of taxes, Matthew heard from the inspector that the amount of income tax repayment due to Mrs Blake's estate was £46.90 (the amount of tax deducted at 20% from the Coats Viyella dividend). He agreed this and applied to the inspector for repayment (which, when he received it, he would pay into the executors' account). He told the inspector that he expected the administration of the estate to be completed very shortly and requested from the inspector the executors' income tax return for the period from the date of death until 5 April 1998.

Matthew then realised that the legacy of £200 payable to Help the Aged was exempt because it was a gift to a charity. This would reduce IHT by £80 (40% on £200). Matthew wrote again to the Capital Taxes Office, advising them that although there was an income tax refund of £46.90 due to the estate he had forgotten to allow for the legacy to a charity. He also realised there would be a refund of IHT of £61.24 (£80 less £18.76 being 40% of £46.90). He could now write to the Inland Revenue to apply for Form IHT 30.

Form IHT 30 is the formal application to the Inland Revenue for a certificate that all IHT has now been paid on the assets disclosed. However, if the executor has been able to take advantage of the ten annual instalments option, the certificate will be qualified and restricted to property on which IHT has been paid in full. Where this is the case, it could be ten years before the final Form IHT 30 is issued, when all the instalments of tax on the estate have been paid.

Selling some of the shares

Matthew knew that he had to set aside £450 to pay the legacies (£50 to each of the three grandchildren, £100 to Alison Ward and £200 to Help the Aged). There was also the mortgage and other debts to pay off, as well as the rest of the IHT. Matthew knew that the mortgage would be paid off from the life policy proceeds, but having discussed it with Robert and Emma they decided to sell some shares because, although Mark would get the house, Robert and Emma each wanted some spare cash. If they had retained all the shares in the estate they could later have sold any of them, but would have lost the opportunity to make gains exempt from capital gains tax in the estate, and the gains would have to be counted against their own personal capital gains tax exemptions. Where the market for shares has fallen generally this can be a valuable relief if some shares have to be sold.

So Matthew, having discussed it with Robert and Emma, decided to sell as many shares as was necessary to raise approximately £17,000. He decided to sell the small holdings first (most of which happened to have gone up in value since the date of death), so he sold the Coats Viyella, Alliance Trust, Monks Investment, BAT and Marks & Spencer shares, through the bank, sending sealed copies of the probate and the certificates for the company registrars. The bank let him have a stock transfer form for each holding, and Matthew and Robert signed them.

It is not advisable to sell shares direct without a broker. When it is done through the bank, it is the bank's broker who does the actual selling. If Matthew or Robert had been in the habit of buying and selling shares, they would have gone to one of their own brokers. If a broker is used, find out his commission rates before giving dealing instructions. Selling through a bank's broker attracts a commission just as any other broker, often with a minimum fee of, say, £15 per holding. The bank may also charge a dealing fee.

The formalities for selling and transferring government stock (so called gilt-edged) are very similar to ordinary shares, but the registrar is the Bank of England.

The sales of Mary Blake's shares raised a total of £17,543.16 after deduction of commission and fees. This amount bears no direct relation to the value of the shares at the date of death but is the result of the price of shares on the day of sale. The money was sent to Matthew ten days later, and he paid it into the executorship account.

He made a note of the prices at which the shares were sold and the net proceeds of each after dealing costs, to compare with the value at the date of Mrs Blake's death, in case there should be liability for capital gains tax.

Paying off the other creditors

There were no further assets to collect in. Matthew had now received all moneys due to the estate. After the proceeds of sale from the stocks and shares were received, on 3 September, and the income tax repayment of £46.90, and after the bank charge (£25) for dealing with the indemnity for the replacement of the Coats Viyella share certificate, the balance on the executors' bank account was £30,208.20. This was a large amount to have on a bank current account so Matthew wrote the following letter to the bank:

[Date]

Dear Sirs,

Executors of Mary Blake

Please take this letter as my authority and instruction to you to open a deposit account in the names of the executors of Mary Blake and to transfer at the end of each banking day either to or from the deposit account sufficient to leave £1,000 to the credit of the current account.

Yours faithfully,

In this way he knew that there would be money available for cheques to meet the debts, but also that the money would be earning interest. He sent the letter to Robert for his signature before posting it to the bank.

He then wrote to the Minford Building Society:

[Date]

Dear Sirs,

Mary Blake (deceased)

Probate has now been granted so I enclose herewith a sealed copy of the probate with the signed claim form for the Immortal Life Policy. Could you please arrange to discharge the mortgage from the proceeds and send me the balance due, together with a statement accounting for the interest on the life policy proceeds and the mortgage to the date of discharge.

On 17 September he received a letter back from the building society enclosing the following statement:

Proceeds of endowment Life Policy: Immortal Life Assurance Society as at 10 April 1997	38,761.50	Mortgage account at date of death	25,124.35
Interest paid net after deduction of income Tax at basic rate	1,130.52	Interest since date of death to 15 September	2,048.72
Total proceeds	£39,892.02		£27,173.07

Balance due to you cheque herewith £12,718.95

Enclosed herewith also the Income Tax Deduction certificate as follows:

Total interest	1,507.36
Tax deducted	376.84
Interest paid	£1,130.52

He then wrote a letter back to them:

[Date]

Dear Sir,

Re: Mary Josephine Blake deceased, The Firs, Willow Lane, Minford

Further to your letter please send all the deeds and documents to me, together with the official certificate of discharge.

On the question of insurance for the building, we wish to continue the existing policy, but to have it transferred to the name of Mr Mark Douglas Blake (to whom the property has been devised), and to take the opportunity of increasing the cover to £97,500. Will you please arrange this (and let me know the increase in premium), or put me in touch with the insurance company so that I can do so.

Yours faithfully,

Matthew paid the cheque into the bank account and kept the tax certificate for later.

He then arranged to pay the other debts including the gas bill, telephone account, garage and wines and spirits bills, and he also paid the undertaker's bill. These were as listed in Form IHT 44.

Another task was to deal with the hire purchase on the dishwasher. He had written to the finance company soon after his mother-in-law's death to explain that no instalments could be paid until after the grant of probate was obtained. He now decided that the easiest thing to do was to pay all the outstanding instalments in one. Rather than go through the paraphernalia of continuing the hire purchase agreement in the name of Mrs Blake's son, he sent to the finance company a cheque for what was outstanding – £46.20 – plus £1 for the actual purchase of the machine. He got a receipt, and there was no further difficulty.

He could, if he had preferred, have arranged for the agreement to be continued in Mark Blake's name, or put it into the names of the executors, in which case he would still have paid the instalments out of the estate.

Form IHT 30

Matthew was now ready to deal with the final adjustments of IHT, after which he would be in a position to complete and submit Form IHT 30 confirming the IHT liability of the estate.

First, Matthew considered those assets on which IHT had to be paid immediately. The total already paid was £13,319.98 but to this figure he added the £18.76 arising on the refund of tax. He then deducted the IHT of £80, being the tax he had inadvertently paid on the charitable legacy of £200. Overall, a refund of £61.24 was due.

Next, he considered the house. On the original valuation of £125,000 the tax payable was £16,197.47 but to this sum he would have to add another £1,000, being the tax assessed on the increased value of £2,500.

Matthew submitted these adjustments to the Capital Taxes Office, after which he received revised assessments for the IHT due immediately (on which there was a refund).

He could now complete two copies of Form IHT 30. One copy would be returned to him with the completed certificate as an acknowledgement that the Capital Taxes Office was satisfied, on the information provided, that no further IHT was due on the personal estate.

Where an election has been made to pay IHT by instalments, an application can still be made for a clearance certificate but, when it is returned, Inland Revenue will note on it that it applies only to those assets on which IHT has been paid in full.

There were no other material facts, such as trusts or settlements, so Matthew and Robert signed both copies of Form IHT 30 and sent them to the Capital Taxes Office.*

Although it says on Form IHT 30 that it should not be submitted until the applicant has reason to believe that no adjustment to the amount of inheritance tax paid will be necessary, if an asset or a debt should, after all, be disclosed later, the matter can be re-opened.

It is only when the second copy of Form IHT 30, with the certificate signed and stamped, is returned, that the personal representatives can safely proceed to distribute the money they have in hand to those entitled to it, secure in the knowledge that the Capital Taxes Office will not later be claiming more tax.

The Form IHT 30 has the effect of fixing the value of assets conclusively as at the date of death. If a sale of a house, for example, is expected to raise a much larger figure than that disclosed or agreed with the district valuer, it may be taken as an indication that a higher valuation should have been put on the particular asset concerned. So it may be prudent, in such a case, to wait until Form IHT 30 is obtained before going ahead with the sale, because until Form IHT 30 is obtained the question of value can be re-opened.

Transferring the shares

Matthew and Robert had now collected in all the monies due to the estate and paid all the debts. They now had to distribute all the property in accordance with the will. The first item to be dealt with was the remaining shares Mrs Blake had owned.

It is often necessary to sell some or all of the shares held by a person who has died in order to pay the debts, IHT or the legacies or to meet the expenses of administering the estate. Where this happens, as in Matthew's case, it is then the remaining shares which get divided according to the will.

Where shares or unit trust holdings are sold within a year of a death, for less than the value on the date of death, the total of the gross selling price of all such investments sold within the year can be substituted for the value for IHT. The sale has to be made by the executors; once the shares have been transferred into the names of the beneficiaries, it is too late to claim a reduction of IHT. Adjustment is made by a corrective document. Where the market for shares has fallen generally, this can be a valuable relief if some shares have to be sold.

Whether the shares are sold or not, it is necessary for each company in which shares are held to see a copy of the probate. A letter addressed to the registrar of the company at the head office will always ultimately reach the right destination, but Matthew had already found out the names and addresses of the registrars when he wrote to them to confirm the holdings.

In a case where a sole executor is also the person entitled to the shares under the will, no formal transfer of the shares is usually needed. Instead, a document called a letter of request (Form CON41A published by Oyez Stationery) can be used.

Where the shares are to be sold, or where (as in Mrs Blake's case) the shares are to be transferred direct to the beneficiaries entitled to have them under the will, it is usually possible to send the probate to the registrar of the company at the same time as sending the transfers of the shares to be dealt with by him.

Dividing up shares

The unsold shares comprised part of the residue of the estate – not having been left to anyone else. This meant that, under the will, Mrs Blake's two children, Emma and Robert, were entitled to the shares equally. It would therefore be necessary to value the shares again if they were not dividing every shareholding because their relative worth would have changed since the date of death, and Emma and Robert were entitled to equal value as at the date the administration was ended. Administration ends when all debts are paid and all the taxes dealt with including those for the period of administration. If the beneficiaries do not split the actual holdings, a valuation is needed as at the date of completion of administration, and the administration or estate account should show this.

Mrs Blake had owned investments of a kind which, in normal times, Matthew might well have chosen, if asked to advise on the subject. He suggested that the two children who were entitled to the residue of the estate should divide and should take over, as they stood, the unsold investments which their mother had held, and they agreed.

It is perfectly possible to divide up each existing holding of shares. One way – perhaps the fairest if there is any prospect of disagreement or resentment – is to divide each holding among the beneficiaries. Then each one gets exactly the same. This is what Robert and Emma, on Matthew's advice, decided to do.

Alternatively, the beneficiaries can agree in writing who is to take over what shares on what day, using the Stock Exchange closing prices as shown in the financial columns of the national press. Fine adjustments, needed to achieve exact divisions, can be made out of any cash balance in hand. If no agreement is possible, all the shares should be sold and the beneficiaries then get their entitlement in cash. Then there can be no argument about who gets what, but from an investment point of view this may not be the most advantageous thing to do.

It can happen with unit trusts that the amount held is such that the manager of the fund will not split it because the split holding would be below the minimum holding allowed or would not be of the correct denomination (for example, some funds specify that holdings must be in multiples of 50 units). In such a case it may be easiest either to sell the whole holding, or to transfer the whole holding to one or other of the beneficiaries, and make a cash adjustment to compensate the other beneficiary, so that they all end up receiving an equal share of the estate.

Formalities of transferring shares

Matthew took the share certificates, together with the copies of the probate, to the Minford branch of Barminster Bank, and asked the manager to deal with them. Where executors employ the bank to lodge the transfers for registration, they may as well let the bank do the whole thing, merely sending the certificates to the bank manager with appropriate detailed instructions (about who is to get what) for the necessary action.

The bank would debit the executorship account with any fees. Some banks do not charge, treating it as a courtesy service to their customers; others charge between £2 and £6 per share, but this fee includes the service of providing and completing the transfer forms and submitting them to the registrars.

It is also possible to obtain transfer forms (called CON 40) from an Oyez shop and to complete them for each of the shares held and send them to the companies concerned so that the beneficiaries can be registered as the new owners. This form has to be completed by putting the name of the company concerned or the unit trust or gilt-edged stock, as appropriate, and specifying the number of the holding and the particular type of the security ('Ordinary shares of 25p each').

A separate form must be used for each different transferee, so in Matthew's case there were two separate transfer forms for each holding because half of the holding was going to Robert and half to Emma. There is a space where names of the present owners, the transferors, have to be inserted. In this case, it was the executors. Although on the company's register the shares may still be in the name of Mary Blake, the registrars will accept the transfer in the executors' names provided a sealed copy of the probate is sent at the same time. As far as the registrar is concerned, the sealed copy probate operates as the transfer from Mary Blake to the executors.

The full name and address of the transferee (Robert or Emma, as appropriate) had to be entered on each of the stock transfer forms, so that there will be one set of transfer forms in favour of Emma and a separate set of transfer forms in favour of Robert.

In Mary Blake's estate, the bank dealt with all this for them and the total charge came to £55.

There is no longer any stamp duty payable on shares transferred from executors to beneficiaries provided that there is endorsed on the transfer form a certificate in the following terms: 'I hereby certify that this instrument falls within category ... of the Schedule to the Stamp Duty (Exempt Instruments) Regulations 1987'. Where the shares are a specific legacy, it is category 'B'; where they are part of the residuary estate, it is category 'E'; where they are transferred by way of entitlement under the intestacy rules, it is category 'C'.

Eventually, Matthew received back the sealed copies of the probate and some time later the new share certificates showing Mrs Blake's two elder children as the owners of their new holding of shares. This was proof of ownership of the shares.

Capital gains tax

Matthew had to consider the capital gains tax position. This is payable when assets are sold for a higher price than they cost when they were bought or higher than their probate value, that is their valuation at the time of the owner's death. (The cost, or base value, can be raised in line with the rise in the retail prices index, and so any gain may be reduced.)

When shares are to be transferred to the beneficiaries and they are showing a gain since the date of death, it might be better to sell the shares within the estate, give cash to the beneficiaries and for the beneficiaries then to buy back the shares with the cash: they then obtain a higher base value for any future sale. If a beneficiary is paying 40% on his top slice of income his CGT rate will be the same, whereas the executor's rate will be 25%.

Every person is allowed a certain amount of gains in each tax year (from 6 April to the following 5 April) without paying any tax, and any losses can be offset against any gains. In April 1997 this exempt amount was raised to £6,500. The executors of an estate also have the annual exemption, £6,500 per year, independently of the beneficiaries who are entitled to the assets. This offers considerable scope for avoiding or lessening gains, and utilising losses, to be offset against gains. The £6,500 exemption for executors is available for the tax year in which the deceased died, and for each of the two following tax years. If, therefore, the beneficiaries are likely to have their own gains in any of these years, it might be better for the executor to continue to hold the shares in the administration of the estate, and if they need to be sold at a gain, which would be taxable if the beneficiaries had owned the shares, the executors can use part of the £6,500 exemption. An indexation allowance is also available unless its use creates or increases a capital loss.

Treasury or Exchequer stock and similar so-called 'gilts' are exempt from capital gains tax.

In Matthew's case, the shares which had been sold had all shown slight gains, but the total gain was well within the £6,500 exemption. Some of those which were transferred to Robert and Emma were showing losses. If the beneficiaries had taxable gains in that tax year against which these losses could have been offset, the executors could have sold the shares in Robert's and Emma's names and offset the losses. However, there was none, so Robert and Emma took over the higher base value at the date of Mary Blake's death.

Where the gains are likely to be more than £6,500, it may be thought prudent to take professional advice as to how to minimise capital gains tax payable. The sale could, in such a case, perhaps be split between the executors and the beneficiaries in such a way that there would be more than one £6,500 exemption available for any one tax year. Matthew here just had to make a record of those sold within the administration for the purposes of the income tax return.

In Mary Blake's estate, the house will be transferred to Mark. Where, as often happens, the house has to be sold, capital gains tax will be assessed on the rise in value since the date of death, based on the probate value. Where a property is sold for less than the probate value within four years of the death the sale price may be substituted for the probate value. All costs such as estate agents and legal costs can be deducted and there is also an indexation allowance. Any gain will be liable to CGT subject to the executor's £6,500 nil-rate exemption which relates to all sales in the tax year concerned. The disposal showing the costs and net gain would have to be included in the executors' tax return.

Transfer of the house

Where a mortgage is outstanding at the time of death and there is nothing in the will about having it paid off out of the residue, the house may have to be sold so that the mortgage can be paid off out of the proceeds of the sale and the beneficiary would get the balance of the money. (But, as with Mary Blake, many people nowadays have a mortgage protection policy or a mortgage on an endowment policy basis, so that the mortgage can be repaid automatically on the death of the borrower.) Where the house is going to be transferred outright into the name of a beneficiary, the building society may be prepared to let the beneficiary continue with the existing mortgage, or would probably grant a new mortgage. He can, of course, apply to any source – another building society, for example, or bank – for a loan.

Registered property

The title to the house was a registered one. It was not strictly accurate, therefore, of Matthew to have spoken of the deeds of the house when he wrote to the Minford Building Society, although it is common practice even in the legal profession to do so. He really meant the charge certificate, which the building society held as part of its security for the money it had lent. When a house has a registered title, and a mortgage on it is completely paid off, the building society hands back the charge certificate to the owner, together with an official acknowledgement that the money due under the mortgage has been paid. This acknowledgement is usually on a special Land Registry form, known as Form 53. The owner then sends the charge certificate, together with Form 53, to the Land Registry. Some time later he receives from the registry the land certificate, which is substantially the same as the charge certificate, but with the important difference that the details of the mortgage have been officially crossed out. In this way, the owner obtains formal proof of his ownership, free from any mention of a mortgage. Even a straightforward case can take several weeks.

It can happen that the property is left in the will to people who have only a life interest, for example where a husband allows his wife to live there for the rest of her life. In this case there will have to be two trustees who will become the owners of the legal title to the property and hold it on trust for the wife. Alternatively, often forms of trust may have been created. In either case there are certain entries which must be made on the Land Registry title and so a solicitor should be consulted.

Mrs Blake was currently registered at the Land Registry as being the owner – or registered proprietor, to use the official expression – of The Firs, Willow Lane, Minford. To prove that the executors now replaced her, the probate would have to be registered with the Land Registry. And there was a further step involved: to transfer the house into Mark Blake's name.

All three transactions could be dealt with in a single application to the Land Registry: crossing off the details of the mortgage, substituting the names of the executors for Mrs Blake's and substituting Mark Blake for the executors.

Matthew received the 'deeds' by registered post: the charge certificate, Form 53 (for the discharge of the mortgage) bearing the seal of the building society, and a number of old papers relating to the property. (There may well be a charge to pay to the building society).

Matthew next prepared the form to transfer the ownership of the house into Mark Blake's name. He obtained from the Oyez shop a copy of Land Registry Form 56 (Assent or Appropriation). He could also have obtained this form from HMSO.*

The document by which personal representatives transfer a house to the person entitled to it under a will or intestacy is usually called an assent (accent on the first syllable), and they are said to assent (accent on the second syllable) to the property vesting in the person entitled to it. Form 56 was not difficult to complete. It asked for the title number; for property, the address is all that is necessary. Unlike many other documents, it had the date first. Then the names of the executors had to be filled in, and the name of 'the late ...' where Matthew wrote in the full name and address of Mrs Blake, widow. In the next space had to be put the name of Mark Douglas Blake, and his address. Each of the two executors had to sign the form in the presence of a witness whose address and occupation also had to be given.

Form 56 can also be used for a leasehold house or flat, in which case the landlord usually has to be notified. Depending on the terms of the lease, he may be entitled to receive a copy of the completed form and to demand a fee. Some care should be taken with leasehold property to ensure that there are no outstanding liabilities.

When Form 56 had been completed, signed by Robert Blake and Matthew, and witnessed, Matthew sent it to the appropriate district office of the Land Registry, with a covering letter:

[Date]

Dear Sirs,

Re: The Firs, Willow Lane, Minford, Surrey

I enclosed a sealed copy of the probate of Mary Josephine Blake's will, charge certificate for 'The Firs', Willow Lane, Forms 53 and 56 and cheque payable to HM Land Registry for £50. Please cancel the mortgage and register Mark Douglas Blake as the new owner.

Please then return the copy of the probate and the land certificate to him.

Yours faithfully,

The £50 fee was for registering the assent to Mark Blake, based on the value of the house (there was no fee to pay for cancelling the mortgage). Land Registry fees are based on the value of the house being dealt with, that is, bought or transferred; where the dealings were not 'for value' (that is, not a sale), an abatement is applied:

Scale 2	value fee	fee
	£	£
	0–100,000	40
	100,001–200,000	50
	200,001–500,000	70
	500,001–1,000,000	100
	1,000,001 and over	200

In the 'statement of value' on the reverse of Form 56, Matthew had to fill in the top panel only, giving the title number of the property and its value, in this case £127,500.

Some months later, Mark received the land certificate in which he appeared as the registered proprietor. The reference to the mortgage to the Minford Building Society had been crossed out. But there was a note in the land certificate that the property might be liable for more IHT. This was a routine formality and not appropriate for a case where the IHT had been paid in full and a clearance certificate issued. At the same time, the Land Registry returned the copy of the probate. Thus Mark

Blake became registered as the owner of the house in substitution for his late mother, and the mortgage was cleared.

This is the procedure which must be followed irrespective of whether the ultimate owner of the property, under the will, is a beneficiary or the executor (or administrator). Even if the property is left wholly to an only executor, Form 56 still needs to be completed, to transfer ownership of the property from the executor in that capacity, to himself as owner absolutely.

Unregistered property

If the title to a house is not registered at the Land Registry, the procedure for transferring the house to the person entitled to it is likely to be less straightforward. To find out whether the title is registered or not, it is necessary to inspect the deeds. If there is no land certificate (or charge certificate at the building society, if the property is mortgaged) with the deeds, it means that the title is not registered. Registration of title has now become compulsory, which means that the titles to properties have to be registered, but only by the purchaser after completing his purchase. The result is that even now many houses still have unregistered titles. It is not necessary to register a title when a house changes hands on a death – only on a sale. If a bundle of deeds has been found, they should be checked to make sure they are not the pre-registration deeds (if they are, they will have a Land Registry stamp on the outside cover).

In the case of an unregistered title, the executor, after paying off the mortgage, if there is one, should find among the deeds and documents one deed which is the conveyance of the property to the deceased when he bought it. (If the house is leasehold, it is called an assignment.) This is the deed prepared at the time the house was bought and which transferred ownership of it to the deceased. If the deceased acquired the property by inheritance the executor will be looking for the assent which put the property into the deceased's name. This deed should be used as the basis for preparing the document to transfer ownership to the person now entitled to it under the will or intestacy. This document is called an assent, the same name as is used in the case of a house with a registered title, and in a simple case can be prepared by the executor alone.

Imagine that Mrs Blake's house had an unregistered title, and that the executors had wished to put the house into Mark Blake's name, now that he was entitled to it. When he had paid off the building society mortgage, Matthew would have received from the building society the title deeds to the house. These would have included the mortgage deed, at the back of which would now appear a receipt, bearing the official seal of the building society, which acknowledged that all the money due had now been paid off, which discharges the mortgage. The Building Society sometimes leaves the date blank, so complete it with the same date as the assent. The title deeds would also have included the deed of conveyance prepared when the house last changed hands on a purchase. Matthew would also have needed the original grant of probate. The assent, on an ordinary sheet of paper, would have read like this:

ASSENT
We hereby assent to the freehold property The Firs, Willow Lane, Minford, Surrey, vesting in Mark Douglas Blake of The Firs, Willow Lane, Minford.
We make this assent as executors of the will of Mrs Mary Josephine Blake who died on 8 April 1997.
Probate of her will was granted to us by the Principal Probate Registry on 9 July 1997.
We hereby acknowledge Mark Douglas Blake's right to the production of the probate.
Dated 1 October 1997.
Signed by the executors of the will of Mary Josephine Blake deceased: Robert Anthony Blake of Wringapeak Farm, Woody Bay, Devon, farmer, and Matthew John Seaton of 14 Twintree Avenue, Minford, education officer.
Signatures: Robert A. Blake M. J. Seaton
Witness: Judy Gurney, The Platt, Amersham
Occupation: Local Government Clerk

In many cases an assent in that form is sufficient. It should not be used where a mortgage has not yet been paid off, and where there are any complications such as restrictive covenants on the property the executor should take legal advice to make sure he is not left with any personal liability for them. In the case of a joint ownership as joint tenants, as a rule, no assent is needed; a death certificate is sufficient to prove the survivor's title and should be placed with the deeds. The form of assent must still be used even where the beneficiary is the only personal representative (or one of several), writing what in effect is an assent to himself.

If the property is a leasehold house the assent should contain a covenant by the beneficiary to observe the terms of the lease, details of the lease should appear in the assent and the landlord should be notified; he may be entitled to a copy of the assent itself and he may demand a fee, depending on the terms of the lease, in the same way as for a registered title. The assent must be signed by the executor and the beneficiary in the presence of a witness who must then add his/her signature, address and occupation.

An assent is not liable for stamp duty, and in the case of unregistered land does not have to be registered anywhere. It has to be put with the deeds, and there it stays.

Registered or unregistered

One formality remains, however, whether the title is registered or not. There should be written or typed on the back of the original grant of probate a brief memorandum giving the essential details of the assent. In the case of Mrs Blake's house, it would have to say something like this:

> Memo: An assent dated 1 October 1997 vested the freehold house The Firs, Willow Lane, Minford, Surrey, in Mark Douglas Blake, and his right to the production of this grant of probate was acknowledged.

Mark Blake, as beneficiary, is given a specific legal right to be shown at any time the original grant of probate, as he may need to when he comes to sell the house, in which case the grant of probate is one of the documents needed to prove his ownership. In this way, anyone who buys the property from Mark is given legal protection, especially against fraud. Matthew then hands the title deeds of the house to Mark, along with the assent, one of the copy probate forms and a death certificate, as these will all be needed by Mark if he comes to sell or mortgage the house in the future. Matthew should also ask Mark to sign a receipt for the deeds.

A difficulty in preparing an assent in the case of unregistered property lies in the fact that there is no one to check it unless and until the property comes to be sold, when the buyer's solicitor will want to look at it. If the executors die before the house comes to be sold and it turns out that the assent was incorrect in some respect, there might be considerable expense and difficulty in putting things right. In the case of registered property, however, the beneficiary knows that the assent is correct as soon as the land certificate, showing him as the new owner, is received back from the Land Registry.

The income tax return

Matthew was now getting near to final distribution, but he knew he could not do this until all income tax and capital gains tax had been settled since the date of death. One problem he had was that income tax would be payable on the interest on the bank deposit account. In order to get a final figure he would have to stop interest running, and close the account. So he wrote to the manager of the bank asking them to close the deposit account, transfer the balance to the current account, including interest to the date on which this was done, and to send to him a statement of both executors' accounts to date. He could then tell what transfers had been made each day, how much was on deposit at any one time, and what the interest added was. The total interest was £875.24. Income tax is payable on this amount because the bank will not deduct tax on interest added to a trust or personal representative's account.

The executors are a separate taxable entity on behalf of the estate. All income in the estate is subject to income tax at the basic rate (currently 25%) and there are no personal reliefs or allowances allowed against the income as there are for individual persons. However, there is one permitted deduction: from the total income received, Matthew could deduct the amount of interest which they had paid to the bank on the loan account for payment of IHT and probate fees. Technically the Inland Revenue could object to a deduction of interest for probate fees, as opposed to IHT, but some inspectors do not take this point.

The executors are also liable for capital gains tax on chargeable gains realised on the sale of assets (including houses) in the estate. In this case, they are allowed the full £6,500 (individual person's CGT nil-rate band) for the year in which the deceased died and the following two years.

When the tax inspector sent back to Matthew the income tax repayment for the period from 6 April 1997 to the date of Mary Blake's death, he also sent the income tax return form (Form R59), to be completed for the first period of the administration of the estate, from 8 April 1997 to 5 April 1998, which was the end of the tax year in which the deceased died. Because all the debts and liabilities had been ascertained by that date, Matthew decided that the administration of the estate was fully complet-ed by 12 October 1997. The administration of an estate is com-pleted as soon as all the assets and liabilities are known and paid; it is irrelevant whether or not the estate has been distributed to the beneficiaries of the will.

If the administration had continued beyond 5 April 1998, Matthew would have had to complete another income tax return form for the next tax year (6 April 1998 to 5 April 1999) for all the income and capital gains up to the date when the administration was finally completed.

The income tax return itself is fairly straightforward to com-plete. It is not necessary to enter on the form the income earned by the estate which had already had income tax deducted from it. During the administration Matthew and Robert had received a number of dividend cheques from the various companies, each of which had attached to it a certificate that income tax had been deducted and paid to the Revenue automatically at 20%. Matthew had sent the cheques, after detaching the certificates attached, to the bank, and the bank had credited these to the executors' account. The total amount of dividend which had been received on the various shares was £327.49 (plus the £205.80 for the 'xd' Stonehill Holdings plc, which he had also sent to the bank; see page 109).

There was also £1,135.66 of interest added to the account at the Rockley Building Society since the date of death, but again this is deemed already to have had 25% income tax deducted from it.

Calculation of income tax in the estate

Matthew now had to calculate the income tax payable on the estate. The only taxable item was the bank interest of £875.24, because everything else had tax already deducted. With the last statement from the bank they had enclosed the Tax Deduction Certificates as proof that tax had been paid. Matthew sent these along with the completed Form R59 to the inspector of taxes. Matthew entered the figure of £875.24 under the heading 'Bank interest and other income received without deduction of income tax'.

The tax was calculated as follows:	
Total gross interest	£875.24
Less interest on executors' loan a/c for IHT	£235.14
Taxable income	£640.10
Tax at 25%	£160.02

One income tax matter which did concern Matthew was the interest which he had paid on the bank loan for inheritance tax and probate fees. He had made a note that this was £235.14. So he claimed a credit from the Revenue of 25% of the £235.14 interest paid to the bank, which was £58.78.

Capital gains tax

The other matter that needed to be dealt with on the income tax return form was to complete the information required for capital gains tax. For this, Matthew made a note on a separate sheet of paper of:

- all the shares that had been sold
- the date of the sales
- the value of those shares as declared in Form IHT 44, and
- the proceeds of sales of each of the individual shares after the various costs and commissions had been deducted.

He came to a figure for the gain on all the sales during the period from the date of the death to 12 October 1997 of £1,180.40, which he entered in the income tax return. Alongside this he wrote 'see schedule attached (exempt, less than £6,500)'.

The last tax matters

All the other entries were 'none' but there were one or two other sections to complete simply to explain that this was a case of an administration of an estate. The form only required one signature, so Matthew completed this and sent it to the inspector of taxes with a letter:

[Date]

Dear Sir,

Re: The estate of Mary Josephine Blake deceased

I enclose the income tax return for the period to 12 October 1997, the date on which the administration of the estate was formally completed, so there will be no further income earned in this estate.

I enclose, however, a copy of a letter from my bank certifying that interest was paid on an executors' loan account for the purposes of paying inheritance tax and I enclose some certificates of tax credit on dividends received in the estate and claim the repayment due to the estate of £58.78 being income tax at the basic rate (25%) on the interest on the loan (£235.14).

I calculate the tax payable to be £160.02 after giving the credit for the interest on the executors' loan account and I enclose the executors' cheque for this amount. Please confirm that all income and capital gains tax matters have been finalised so that I may distribute the estate.

Please send me Forms R185 E for the two residuary beneficiaries of the estate.

Yours faithfully,

Matthew then sent it all to Robert so that Robert would sign the cheque and forward it to the inspector of taxes at the address shown on the form as the office which had issued the form.

Two weeks later Matthew heard from the Inland Revenue who returned the dividend payment counterfoils which were the estate's evidence of tax credit. These would be necessary when preparing the final distribution of cash to the beneficiaries and sending to them the tax deduction certificates for income tax paid in the estate on income received. The Inland Revenue confirmed, as requested, that they had now closed their file.

Distribution according to the will

Little now remained for Matthew to do before all matters were completed. Having made sure that all expenses and all debts had been paid, he was in a position to make a final distribution.

All the expenses involved in the administration of the estate had been paid out of the executorship account at the bank. These expenses included the cost of copies of the probate, the bank's charge on the transfer of shares and the Land Registry fees relating to the transfer of the house. His own out-of-pocket expenses, on postage and such matters as fares to London to visit the Probate Registry, were refunded out of the executorship account, and so were Robert Blake's expenses as the other executor. Personal representatives are not entitled to be paid for the time they devote to the administration of the estate, unless the will specifically says so. But, on the other hand, they are not expected to dip into their own pockets. Matthew had used Mrs Blake's £18.40 cash on travel, stamps and such like; the rest of the expenses, including the jewellery valuation, came to £27.24.

The personal effects

The will left 'furniture and effects' in the house to Mark. He took them over with the house itself, including the three paintings, and they became his property without any formalities. Matthew asked him to write a letter addressed to the executors, confirming that the furniture and effects and car were now in his possession as owner, and were no longer part of the estate. A car may or may not be covered by the expression personal effects; normally it would be, but it is much better, in a will, to make clear the testator's intention by dealing with a car specifically, as Mrs Blake had done.

Receipts

The executors were now in a position to pay the legacies and distribute among the beneficiaries the specific bequests. Robert and Matthew signed the cheques on the executorship account for the pecuniary legacies which Mrs Blake had given in her will. They obtained a receipt from each of the beneficiaries. Mrs Ward's read as follows:

> Mary Josephine Blake deceased
> I acknowledge that I have received the sum of one hundred pounds (£100) from Matthew J. Seaton and Robert A. Blake in settlement of the legacy due to me under the will of my late friend, Mary J. Blake.
> Dated: 9 November 1997
> Signed: *Alison Ward (Mrs)*

The will had also provided that Josef Samson should receive the carriage clock which had belonged to Mary Blake. Matthew wrote to tell him about this and when Mr Samson came to collect the clock, obtained from him this acknowledgement:

> Mary Josephine Blake deceased
> I acknowledge that I have received the carriage clock left to me by the will of the late Mrs Mary Blake.
> Dated: 12 November 1997,
> Signed: Josef R. Samson

Children under 18

As far as the £50 legacies to each of the grandchildren were concerned, there was no problem about any over 18 years old. So far as those under 18 were concerned, there arose the legal difficulty that money or property cannot validly be handed over to a minor – even a 17-year-old. A person under 18 does not have the legal capacity to give the executors a receipt. So there is always the risk that any minor who received his money before being of age might spend it on some frivolous purchase and then demand his money again after his 18th birthday.

The £50 could not be paid to the young grandchildren directly. The executors, therefore, had to invest the money until each child, on becoming 18, could receive his or her share (plus the interest it had earned meanwhile).

Matthew and Robert opened deposit accounts for the three grandchildren in their own names. Because the grandchildren will not earn enough income to pay tax, they can have the interest on the account paid without any tax deducted. To do this they must complete a 'self-certification' form available from banks and building societies. It would be possible for the executors to pay out the interest for the children's benefit, but Matthew and Robert thought that it would be better for it to accrue in the account until they each became of age.

Where an administration is long and complicated, it is possible that the legacies will not be paid for several years. When the legacy is then paid, the legatee receiving the legacy is entitled not only to the actual amount of the legacy but also to interest at 6% per annum from the date one year after the date of death until payment of the legacy. This is taxable as income in the hands of the recipient, but it is deductible against any income earned in the administration for income tax purposes.

The last steps

Matthew was about to take the conclusive step in the administration, the final distribution of the residue. All the other property had been distributed and all that was left was the money in the bank account. Personal representatives should consider carefully everything they have done before parting with the remaining assets.

Matthew went through everything that he had done in connection with the executorship from the moment his mother-in-law had died some six months before. He looked again at every asset in the estate, he looked at each debt, and at each expense, to see that everything had been done properly. This is important if several people are sharing the residue, and it would have been more important still if there had been any dissent within the family. He also asked his fellow executor Robert Blake to look over the papers. Reviewing all his actions over the previous months, Matthew found everything to be in order. So he now set about preparing the estate accounts.

The accounts of the estate

It is not necessary that these accounts should take any particular form as long as they are clear. It is useful to have a separate note of the income received so that the calculation of the tax credit due to each beneficiary is more straightforward.

Matthew knew that the accounts were correct because the balance in the distribution account for the total amount in the bank account was £48,011.87, the same as the last bank statement, which Matthew had received from the bank on the executors' account. This therefore showed him that he still had the correct amount of money left. If these figures are not the same, something is wrong and you would have to look at everything – starting with the adding-up.

The estate of Mary Josephine Blake (deceased)

Estate accounts for period of administration
Date of death 8/4/97 administration completed 12/10/97

CAPITAL ACCOUNT

Receipts	£	£
Assets at date of death		
Property 'The Firs'	127,500.00	
Less mortgage	25,124.35	102,375.65
Endowment life policy, Immortal		
Life Assurance Society		38,761.50
Contents 'The Firs' including jewellery		5,835.00
Life policy, Bridstow Insurance		9,068.97
Premium bonds		1,500.00
Building Society account at date		
of death, Capital		16,727.48
Current account at Barminster Bank		
at date of death		193.52
Cash		18.40
National Savings Bank account		389.20
National Savings Certificates		742.50
Pension from employer	28.30	
State pension	41.07	69.37
Income tax repayments to date of death		46.90
Stocks and shares as disclosed to Inland		
Revenue on Form IHT 44		75,686.98
Gain on stocks and shares sold		3,404.41
Surplus from income account		1,254.60
		£256,074.48

Payments		
Debts outstanding at date of death	227.06	
Option on dishwasher	1.00	228.06
Funeral account paid		1,200.00
Probate fees		601.50
Inheritance tax paid	13,268.81	
less refund	80.00	13,188.81
Banker's charges for guarantee	25.00	
for dealing with shares	55.00	80.00
Land Registry fees		50.00
Executors' expenses		45.64
Legacies paid		450.00
Bequest: carriage clock – value		200.00
Bequest: brooch – value		250.00
Bequest: jewellery – value		1,120.00
Balance to distribution account		238,660.47
		256,074.48

Approved:

....
MATTHEW SEATON   *ROBERT BLAKE*

....
EMMA SEATON   *MARK BLAKE*

INCOME ACCOUNT

Receipts	gross	tax credit/ tax paid	received
	£	£	£
National Savings Bank account	1.94		1.94
Dividend due at date of death on Stonehill Holdings plc	257.25	51.45	205.80
Other dividends received since date of death	436.65	87.33	349.32
Building society account interest added since date of death – June 1997 to close	934.98	233.14	701.24 ⎫
	579.23	144.81	434.42 ⎬
Interest on endowment policy	1,507.36	376.84	1,130.52
Bank interest on executors' deposit account	875.24*	218.81	875.24*
	1,112.38		
Less tax credit on executor's loan		58.78	
Total tax credit available in estate for deduction certificate R185E		£1,053.60	
			£3,698.48

Payments	£
Interest on executors' loan account	235.14
Interest to close mortgage account 'The Firs'	2,048.72
Income tax payable	160.02
Balance to capital account	1,254.60
	£3,698.48

* These figures are the same because the bank paid gross without deducting tax; all the others had tax deducted at source (except the National Savings Bank figure, which is tax-exempt).

DISTRIBUTION ACCOUNT

Receipts

Capital account balance			238,660.47

Payments

		£	£
To Mark			
'The Firs'		127,500.00	
Contents (excluding clock and jewellery)		4,265.00	131,765.00
To Robert			
Half shares retained at value as at date of death		29,441.80	
Half executors' bank account on completion of administration		24,005.93	53,447.73
To Emma			
Half shares retained at value as at date of death		29,441.80	
Half executors' bank account on completion of administration		24,005.94	53,447.74
			238,660.47

In the capital account, he included only the capital balance in the building society account at the date of death. The income account therefore includes the interest accrued to the date of death but not yet added in the first payment of interest added after the date of death (£701.24). The other interest payment (£434.42) represents the further interest due to the date of closing the account.

In the income account, Matthew included the receipts of all the income received after the date of death even if they had been included in the original inheritance tax return on Form IHT 44, so they were excluded from the capital account to avoid recording the same item twice.

He hoped that the way he had drawn up the accounts could readily be understood as showing what had happened to all the estate since the date of death, and sent them to Robert, Emma and Mark for their approval. They signed them and returned them to him. If he had been worried that a beneficiary might challenge his accounts he could have arranged for them to be professionally audited as a precaution.

Income tax again

The only other item was the income tax deduction certificates in Form R185E. Part of the cash which Robert and Emma (who were entitled to the residuary estate) would receive was income earned in the estate. The estate had paid income tax at the basic rate (23%) on all of the income except that part of it taken up by the interest paid to the bank on the bank loan for the inheritance tax and probate fees. The total tax credit, or tax paid, in the estate was £1,053.60 so that each beneficiary, being entitled to half of the estate, was entitled to an income tax credit of £526.80 to the nearest penny.

Matthew completed the certificates in Form R185E as indicated on the forms. The 'trust' referred to was 'the estate of Mary Blake deceased'; the income was the 'gross income from which tax has been deducted'. In the second column he entered the tax deducted and in the last column the net income. He decided to split the dividend income from the other income as the interest rates were 20% for the dividends but 25% for the remainder.

He was able to calculate all the amounts necessary because he knew the figure for the tax credit. The amount of the tax credit is 25% of the gross income paid to the beneficiary from the estate, and the net income is the amount left (75%) when the tax of 25% has been deducted from the gross income. The rate for dividends was 20%.

Matthew then signed the forms, ready to send them to Robert and Emma.

Inheritance Act claims

Certain people can claim a share in the estate if they feel they have not been given 'reasonable provision' by the deceased's will or even by the rules operating on intestacy.

The rules of the Inheritance (Provision for Family and Dependants) Act 1975 state that a claim must be made within six months after the date probate is granted (unless there are some very special circumstances, in which case the time limit may be extended by the court). If there is any question at all that someone may make a claim, the safest thing to do is therefore not to distribute the estate until at least six months have passed since the date of probate.

In Matthew's case, the family had no dispute and there were no people who had previously been divorced or (another) son or daughter excluded from the will, or any such matter. He therefore felt quite happy to distribute the estate even though the full six months had not yet elapsed since probate, and even though the accounts showed that Mark was to receive a benefit of more than £131,000 from the estate, whereas Robert and Emma each were to receive just under £54,000. This in itself could possibly be a reason for Robert and Emma making an application to the court that they had not had reasonable financial provision because they had not been treated equally with Mark. But a court is reluctant to upset a deceased's will, and the court does not say that mere inequality is unreasonable.

In this particular case the whole family felt that the provision was reasonable because Mark had always lived in The Firs and was younger than Robert and Emma and had yet to establish himself properly in life. By contrast, Robert and Emma were already settled and had secure incomes and their own homes and it was therefore inconceivable that any such claim, if it were made, would be successful.

The residue

With Form R185E, Matthew sent to each of Emma and Robert a copy of the signed accounts and the cheques, for which he asked them to sign a formal acknowledgement. When the cheques were cleared, there would be nothing left in the executors' account. He would tell the bank to close the account when all the cheques had been cleared.

In this way, the administration by the executors was brought to an end. Matthew bundled all the papers together, including the original probate and the signed copy of the accounts, and put them in a large envelope to be kept in a safe place, theoretically for twelve years (where there are any life interests under any trusts in the will, the papers should then be kept for twelve years after final distribution following the death of anyone with a life interest). The probate should be handed to Mark when it is no longer needed in connection with the estate, as it remains a key part of Mark's title to the property.

The administration of the estate was now over.

CHAPTER 7

DISTRIBUTION ON INTESTACY

The procedure adopted by personal representatives is broadly the same whether they are executors (appointed in a will) who apply for a grant of probate, or administrators (on an intestacy) who apply for a grant of letters of administration. But there is little point in a relative applying for letters of administration if the estate is insolvent.

When it comes to distributing the estate, the executors follow the directions of the deceased according to the will; administrators must apply the intestacy rules laid down in the Administration of Estates Act 1925.

The nearest relatives, in a fixed order, are entitled to apply for the grant. If the nearest relation does not wish to apply, he can renounce his right to do so, in which case the next-nearest becomes entitled to be the administrator, and so on, down the line of kinship.

The widow, or widower, is primarily entitled to be the administrator. If there is no surviving spouse, or if he or she does not apply for a grant, then any of the children may apply. Grandchildren may apply, if their parents are dead. Next, the deceased's parents may apply, and then brothers and sisters, or their children. They are followed by half-brothers and half-sisters, or their children. Next grandparents, followed by uncles and aunts (or their children) may apply, finishing up with uncles and aunts of the half blood, or their children. No relations remoter than those are legally next of kin so as to be entitled to apply for a grant of letters of administration. A so-called aunt or uncle who is the spouse of a parent's brother or sister does not come into this at all, neither as applying to be the administrator of an intestate estate, nor as a beneficiary from it. In-laws and people related by marriage do not count, only blood-relations.

Until 1970, the only blood relationships which the rules governing intestacy recognised were legitimate ones; an illegitimate person could not claim any interest. Now, no distinction is made between natural, adopted or illegitimate relationships. They are all treated equally. Normally an affiliation order or guardianship order from the court would be required to prove an illegitimate child's claim to his father's estate, but genetic blood testing can now be used if the deceased father's parents are still alive.

An adopted child is deemed to be the legal child of his *adoptive* parents and has exactly the same inheritance right as the adoptive parents' other (natural) children, but loses any rights he may have had in law to his *natural* parents' estate. Similarly, the natural parents of an adopted child lose their rights under intestacy laws. (However, a natural parent can, of course, still benefit such a child in his or her will and *vice versa*.)

The division of the net estate where a person died without leaving a will depends on the value of what is left, and what family survives. The net estate is what remains of the estate after paying the debts, the funeral expenses, the expenses of getting letters of administration, and administering the estate.

Inheritance tax will be payable on the basis of the distribution of the property according to the intestacy rules, i.e. no tax is payable on anything that goes to the surviving spouse. Inheritance tax *is* payable on the balance once the nil-rate band has been used up.

Here are some examples.

If the deceased left a wife or husband

Example A

Deceased's family
Wife and three children.

Net estate
Personal effects (that is, strictly, 'personal chattels', including car – unless it was used for business purposes – furniture, clothing, jewellery and all goods and chattels) and £9,500 (in savings bank, savings certificates). They lived in rented accommodation.

Division of estate under intestacy rules
All to wife, providing she survives her husband by 28 days.

Explanation
The surviving spouse takes the personal effects, no matter how great their value, and the first £125,000 of the rest. In the present example this is less than £125,000, so everything goes to the surviving spouse, and the children get nothing. No other relatives (for example, parents) are entitled to any part of the estate. It would be the same in the case of a wife dying intestate, leaving a husband surviving her.

The rented accommodation has no capital value, although the family is entitled to carry on living there.

Example B

Deceased's family
Wife and three adult children.

Net estate
Personal effects and £185,000 including investments and value of house which was owned solely by the deceased.

Division of estate under intestacy rules

(1) Wife gets:
    (a) personal effects
    (b) £125,000 plus interest on it at 6% per annum from date of death (not, as for a pecuniary legacy under a will, one year from the date of death) until payment
    (c) a life interest in £30,000 (that is, the income from £30,000 for the rest of her life).

(2) Each of the three children gets:
    (a) £10,000 immediately
    (b) £10,000 (or the fund representing the £10,000) on their mother's death.

Explanation

The intestacy rules give the widow all the personal effects, £125,000 (plus interest at 6% from the date of death to the date of payment) and a life interest in half the remainder. The children share half the remainder immediately, and the other half on their mother's death.

. If one of the children had died before the father, leaving any children, then those grandchildren of the deceased would have shared their parent's proportion of their grandfather's estate. It makes no difference if the widow is not the mother of some or all of the children; where, for instance, their father married a second time, the estate is shared as described between the widow and the deceased's children, both her children by him and her stepchildren. Any children or grandchildren under age do not inherit unless and until coming of age or getting married. Other relatives (parents, or stepchildren, of the deceased, for instance) get nothing.

This intestacy creates a very difficult situation for the wife if the value of the house is more than £125,000. In such a case the answer is to create a trust to protect the capital in which the wife has only a life interest. A solicitor should be consulted.

Example C

Deceased's family
Wife and four children; two of them (A and B) are over 18 years old at the deceased's death, and two of them (C and D) are younger than 18.

Net estate
Personal effects and £149,000 made up of £129,000 of investments, and half the value of the house worth £40,000, which was owned as tenants-in-common in equal shares by husband and wife.

Division of estate under intestacy rules
(1) Wife gets:
   (a) personal effects
   (b) £125,000 plus interest on it at 6% per annum from date of death until payment
   (c) a life interest in half the remainder – £12,000 (that is, the income from £12,000 for the rest of her life).
(2) Each of the four children gets:
   (a) £3,000 immediately; A and B will receive their sums immediately; the rest of the money will have to be held by the administrators on trust until C and D respectively reach 18
   (b) on their mother's death, £3,000 (that is, one-quarter of the £12,000 which had been the mother's life interest). The administrators should have invested the amount, so each of the children receives his or her share of the funds representing the £12,000. It may be worth considerably more by that time because the capital may have increased in value although all the income will have been paid to the mother until her death.

Explanation
As for **example B**, but the wife already owns half of the house, so only half the value of the house will be distributed because that is all the deceased owned. The wife may take the other half-share in the house as part of her legacy of £125,000, in which case she could call for the house and become the sole and absolute owner of it. If the house (or the deceased's share of the house) exceeds the amount to which the survivor is entitled under the intestacy rules, she may be able to acquire it by paying the balance to the estate.

Example D

The situation is as for **example C**, but the house was owned by husband and wife as joint tenants. Therefore, regardless of the intestacy rules, the wife acquires the rest of the house automatically and becomes the sole owner. The intestacy rules operate on the rest of the estate only, so the wife gets:

(a) personal effects
(b) £125,000 plus interest on it at 6% per annum from date of death until payment
(c) a life interest in half the remainder – £2,000 (that is, the income from £2,000 for the rest of her life).

The children get £500 each immediately (or on reaching the age of 18), and on their mother's death £500 each (or their equal share of the fund representing their mother's £2,000 life interest).

Example E

Deceased's family
Husband, mother, no children.

Net estate
Personal effects, £32,000 in investments.

Division of estate under intestacy rules
All to husband.

Explanation
Where there are no children, the surviving spouse takes all the personal effects, plus everything else up to £200,000. Mother gets nothing.

Example F

Deceased's family
Wife, mother and father, two brothers, no children.

Net estate
Personal effects, £225,000 in investments and house in sole name of deceased.

Division of estate under intestacy rules
(1) Wife gets:
    (a) personal effects
    (b) £200,000, plus interest on it at 6% per annum from date of death until payment
    (c) £12,500
(2) mother gets £6,250
(3) father gets £6,250.

Explanation
The surviving wife or husband takes the personal effects and £200,000, plus interest until payment. The rest is divided in two; the surviving spouse takes one half, and the other half is divided equally between the deceased's parents (the brothers get nothing). If only one parent had been alive, he or she would have received the whole of the parents' £12,500. If he had no parents living, his brothers would share equally that £12,500; the share of any brother or sister who died before the deceased would be divided equally between his or her children.

Example G

Deceased's family
Husband, no children, no parents, no brothers or sisters, no nephews or nieces, no grandparents; one aunt, four cousins.

Net estate
Personal effects, £240,000 in investments.

Division of estate under intestacy rules
All to husband.

Explanation
If, apart from the surviving spouse, there are no parents or any issue of parents and the nearest relations are aunts, uncles, cousins, or grandparents, the surviving spouse takes everything, no matter how much it is.

If the deceased left no wife or husband

Example H

Deceased's family
No wife, three surviving children, seven grandchildren, two of whom are children of a son who died some years before.

Net estate
£3,500, personal effects to the value of £500; total £4,000.

Division of estate under intestacy rules
(1) Each of the three surviving children gets £1,000 ($\times$ 3 = £3,000)
(2) Each of the two grandchildren whose father died before the deceased gets £500 ($\times$ 2 = £1,000)
(3) The other grandchildren get nothing.

Explanation
Where there is no wife or husband, the whole estate is shared between the children equally. It makes no difference how big or small the estate is. The share of any child who has already died is shared equally between his children; this process of taking a deceased parent's share can go on to the third and fourth generation, if necessary. Any children or grandchildren who are under age do not get a share until they come of age, or marry, and until that time the administrators hold the fund for them as trustees.

Example I

Deceased's family
Two brothers.

Net estate
£3,000 including personal effects.

Division of estate under intestacy rules
£1,500 to each brother.

Explanation
If the parents of a bachelor or a spinster (or widow or widower with-out descendants) are both dead, the whole estate is shared between brothers and sisters equally. The share of a deceased brother or sister goes to his or her children. If a parent had been alive, he or she would have taken everything, and brothers and sisters would have received nothing. If both parents are alive, they share the estate equally.

Relatives of the whole blood take priority over relatives of the half blood. If, for example, a bachelor whose parents are dead has one brother and one half-brother, the brother takes everything and the half-brother takes nothing. But if there is no brother of the whole blood, then a half-brother would take everything in priority to grand-parents, or aunts, uncles or cousins. The same applies to other rela-tives of the half blood: they take only if corresponding relatives of the whole blood (or their descendants) are not alive to inherit a share. An adopted child counts as being a child of the full blood for the purpose of inheritance, and so does any illegitimate relative of the deceased. Relatives by marriage do not count.

Example J

Deceased's family
One aunt, two uncles, three cousins who are children of one deceased uncle, four cousins who are children of one deceased aunt, five cousins who are children of the two living uncles; no children, no parents, no brothers or sisters, no grandparents.

Net estate
£6,000.

Division of estate under intestacy rules

(1) £1,200 each to the aunt and two uncles

(2) £400 each to the three cousins who are children of the deceased uncle

(3) £300 each to the four cousins who are children of the deceased aunt.

Explanation

The aunt and uncles, being the nearest relatives, share the estate equally. But the children of any dead aunt or dead uncle share what the aunt or uncle would have received if he or she had survived long enough. So the estate is divided into five (£6,000 ÷ 5 = £1,200); the one-fifth share of the dead uncle is divided into three equal shares for his children (the three cousins on that side of the family), and the one-fifth share of the dead aunt is divided into four equal shares for the children (the four cousins on that side of the family). The cousins whose relevant parent is still alive get nothing.

It would be essential for the administrators to make sure that they were aware of all possible claimants before distributing the estate. They should therefore place the statutory advertisement in the *London Gazette* (and perhaps local newspapers) – see page 149. It is up to anyone who claims to be a relative to prove that he or she is entitled; this is usually done by showing necessary birth, marriage and death certificates. If the administrators have any doubts at all whether the family tree is complete, they should seek legal advice. The only safe course for them, to guard against the possibility of some remote relative later coming forward, may be to pay the money into court. The court can then discharge them from their duties as administrators and any applicant must therefore apply to the court and show his claim.

Example K

Deceased's family

Five second cousins (relatives who have the same great-grandparents as the deceased).

Net estate

£10,000.

Division of estate under intestacy rules
Everything to the Crown (or the Duchy of Cornwall or the Duchy of Lancaster in those areas).

Explanation
Only relatives who can show that they are descendants of (or are) the deceased's grandparents can take a share in the estate of someone who died intestate. To be a descendant of the deceased's great-grandparent is not sufficient, and if there are no nearer relatives, the estate goes to the Crown. It is then called *bona vacantia*, property to which no one can claim a title. Often the Treasury Solicitor, who administers *bona vacantia*, makes a distribution of some or even all of the net estate, after paying the expenses, among those who can show a strong moral claim: where a distant relative has looked after the deceased for many years, for example, or where a void will has been made which would have left everything to a close friend. This may also happen where the deceased had been living with a woman to whom he was not married. But she is likely to do better by claiming under the Inheritance (Provision for Family and Dependants) Act 1975, since she would count as being someone who 'immediately before the death of the deceased was being maintained either wholly or partly by the deceased'. This rule has recently been relaxed so that financial dependence does not have to be proved. This would give her a right to claim reasonable provision – probably an income, but perhaps a capital sum as well out of the estate. Such a claim should be made without delay. The procedure for this is complicated.

Anyone considering making a claim under the Inheritance Act (on an intestacy or also where there was a will) should certainly consult a solicitor before taking any action. It is possible to lodge a notice at court so as to be notified if any grant of probate or letters of administration is made in any particular person's estate, and thus have notice when the six months' period starts to run. A solicitor will be able to deal with this, and advise how to register such a notice. Advice should therefore be taken as soon as possible, and action can be taken even before the death of the person concerned.

Who inherits the property of an umarried person without children who died intestate

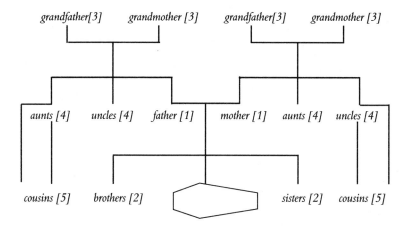

CHAPTER 8

In Scotland, Confirmation

Executors appointed by your will are called executors-nominate. For a person who dies without a will, the court will appoint executors-dative.

Where the deceased died without a will, some member of the family has (except for a small estate, that is an estate whose value before deduction of debts does not exceed £17,000) to petition the court for appointment as executor-dative. Such petitions are best put in the hands of a solicitor.

All executors, whether nominate or dative, have to be officially approved before they can start collecting in the estate. This approval is termed confirmation because the sheriff principal confirms the authority of the people who have been appointed by the will or the court previously.

When an estate is insolvent

If an executor realises that the estate is insolvent, he should not continue with the administration but petition the court straight away for a trustee to be appointed to administer the estate – otherwise, he may become personally liable for the debts.

When no confirmation is needed

It is not always essential to obtain confirmation. The rules for payments of up to £5,000 by organisations such as the Department for National Savings are the same in Scotland as in England and Wales. Confirmation is also unnecessary in the case of property held in common by the deceased and another on a title which contains a survivorship destination. On death, the deceased's share of the property passes to the other automatically, bypassing the executor.

If confirmation is required for even one item, all the assets (even cash, personal effects, furniture, the car and similar items) have to be entered in the inventory for confirmation. The deceased's share of property held in common with another person must also be confirmed to, unless the title to the property contains a survivorship destination (when the share is disclosed for tax purposes only).

First formalities

Executors, whether nominated in the will or appointed by the court, have limited powers before confirmation. In this period, they should confine themselves to safeguarding and investigating the estate. They should not hand over any items to beneficiaries. Any person who interferes with the deceased's property may be held personally liable for all the deceased's debts, however large. The liability of confirmed executors for debts is limited to the value of the estate they confirm to. Executors who are confirmed later also enjoy such limited liability, as long as they acted prudently and within their legal authority before confirmation.

Executors not wishing to act

An executor-nominate (one appointed by the will) who does not wish to act can decline to be confirmed. A simple signed statement to that effect is all that is required. The remaining executor(s) appointed will then be confirmed. It is not possible to decline and nevertheless reserve the right to apply later.

If a sole executor-nominate declines, the estate may be put to the expense of applying to the court for another executor to be appointed. Instead, the nominated executor should bring in someone else as a co-executor and then decline, leaving the co-executor to be confirmed and act alone.

An executor appointed by the court cannot simply decline. He or she has to apply to the court for the appointment to be cancelled. Neither can such an executor bring in co-executors.

If the house was 'joint' property

Property owned by two or more people in Scotland is invariably held in common rather than jointly. Joint holdings are restricted to trustees, or members of clubs or similar institutions.

Where property is held in common, each owner's share forms part of his or her estate on death and is dealt with either by the will or the intestacy rules. What share each owner possesses is stated in the title to the property. Usually the property is shared equally, but this is not always the case. The title to common property may contain a survivorship destination. This will have been agreed and put in the title when the property was acquired.

The effect of a survivorship destination is that the share of the first co-owner to die passes automatically to the survivor. Most married couples put survivorship destination into the title of their home so that the survivor is assured of being able to continue to live there. The survivorship destination does not alter the shares held by the co-owners; that continues to be governed by the shares mentioned in the title.

Joint bank account

There are two main types of joint account. The first type requires both the account holders to sign cheques. The second type, which is more common, is called an 'either or survivor account'. Here either holder can sign cheques while both are alive. On the death of the first holder, the survivor can continue to sign cheques. The type of account, however, regulates only the entitlement of the holder to withdraw and the bank to pay money; it does not determine who owns the money. Ownership depends on who put money into the account and their intentions in doing so. Where only one holder put money in and made the account joint so that the other could also sign cheques, the money remains the property of the contributing holder. On the other hand, if the intention was to pool resources, each holder has a half share of the balance. The law assumes pooling was not intended, so this has to be proved.

Where both holders contributed, the balance is divided according to the contributions made unless this is too difficult to work out or there was an intention to pool, in which case the balance is divided equally.

These rules apply also to most joint accounts held by a married couple. It is perhaps more likely in the case of a husband and wife that their intention was to pool resources, but the presumption against pooling still applies. However, the balance in a 'housekeeping' account is shared equally, unless the couple agreed otherwise.

Confirmation forms

The forms required for obtaining confirmation can be obtained from the Capital Taxes Office,* or H M Commissary Office* or main post offices *and sheriff courts in Scotland. There are no special forms for lay applicants.*

Once you, the executor, have all the information regarding the valuation of various assets in the estate and the deceased's debts, you are ready to fill in the appropriate form for obtaining confirmation.

When there is more than one executor, one of them applies for confirmation on behalf of all. The executors should agree among themselves who is to apply. An executor appointed by the will who does not wish to act must sign a statement to this effect. This statement accompanies the application for confirmation. Executors appointed by the court are not permitted to decline to act; they have to apply to the court for their appointment to be cancelled.

If the estate is under £17,000 in value before debts are deducted, it is a small estate, and there are special procedures that you can use to obtain confirmation. These are set out on pages 200–1, after the normal procedure has been discussed.

Normal procedure

Briefly, the steps are:

(a) complete the appropriate form
(b) take an oath
(c) pay any inheritance tax due
(d) lodge the form and other documents at the sheriff court.

In Scotland there is no special assistance for lay executors except in the case of small estates, and although the staff in the sheriff court are helpful, if you are in difficulty, you should get a solicitor to advise you.

Completing the forms

Depending on the size of the estate, you will need Form A-3 or B-4. Form B-4 may be used where the gross estate does not exceed £145,000 in value, the deceased made no chargeable lifetime transfers, and had no interest in settled property. This sum may change from time to time. Form A-3 is for all other estates which are not small estates.

The first two pages of Forms A-3 and B-4 are identical. You are required to fill in details of the deceased and the appointment of executors. Page 2 also contains formal statements which you have to swear to.

The main part of both forms is the section called the inventory (pages 5–7 on Form A-3 and pages 4 and 5 on Form B-4). Here you list, item by item together with the value of each item, all the estate situated in the United Kingdom and moveable estate situated abroad. Everything the deceased owned must be listed, otherwise any persons holding omitted assets may refuse to hand them over to you.

The items should be listed in the following order:

Estate in Scotland

Heritable estate (that is, land or buildings) is put first. A typical example is the deceased's house if he or she owned it or a share of it. For a house, the postal address is normally a good enough description, but for land you will need to use the formal description in the title deeds. You do not need to include property whose title contains a survivorship destination.

Moveable estate comes afterwards. This includes items such as cash, furniture and personal effects, a car, bank or building society accounts where the branch is in Scotland, national savings investments and government stock, shares in Scottish companies, income tax refund, arrears of pay or pension, and other sums or debts due to the deceased.

Real and personal estate in England and Wales

Real estate (land or buildings) is put first. Personal estate is other types of property such as shares in English companies.

Real and personal estate in Northern Ireland

As for England and Wales.

At this point you summarise the value of the estate under the above headings. This is done to show the amount of estate you are seeking to be confirmed to.

Moveable property outside the United Kingdom

This includes items such as shares in foreign companies.

A sample inventory is shown opposite.

Other sections of the forms ask for details of the deceased's debts, trust property in which the deceased had an interest, foreign land, lifetime gifts made by the deceased, and property (whether in Scotland or elsewhere) passing under a survivorship destination.

Estate in Scotland

		£	
1. House and garden at 6 Napier Road, Edinburgh	£185,000		
Less sum due to Halifax Building Society	25,000		160,000
2. Cash in house			27
3. Furniture, furnishings and personal effects belonging to deceased at 6 Napier Road			7,500
4. VW Passat motor car registration number B318 JSX			1,500
5. Arrears of pay (net) from Scottish Office			650
6. Royal Bank of Scotland plc, 36 St Andrew Square, Edinburgh. Sum at credit of current a/c No. 230556			427
7. Nationwide Building Society, Newington Road, Edinburgh			
Sum at credit of a/c No. 116613972	£153.75		
Interest accrued	3.25		157
8. Standard Life Limited, 3 George Street, Edinburgh. Sum due under Life Policy No. C534712			15,624
9. £2,000 8% Treasury Stock 2003 at 98			1,960
10. Income tax refund		say	1
			£187,846

Estate in England and Wales

	£
11. Rose Cottage, Sea Road, Llangranog	42,000
12. British Telecom plc 400 shares at 201	804
13. Imperial Chemical Industries plc 300 Ordinary shares at £7.25	2,175
	£232,825

Summary for confirmation

Estate in Scotland	£187,846
Estate in England and Wales	£44,979
	£232,825

Moveable estate elsewhere

14. Rank Xerox Inc USA $200 Common Stock at $20=$4,000 converted to sterling value at date of death	£3,121

Form A-3 is more complex than Form B-4. It has an additional page (page 3) with questions about gifts and nominations made by the deceased, joint property in which the deceased had an interest, settled property in which the deceased had an interest, and whether legal rights have been claimed or renounced. It also has a final section concerned with the calculation of inheritance tax payable. The Capital Taxes Office* will help you if you find this section difficult.

Taking the oath

Next you have to swear on oath to the completeness and accuracy of the information given in the form and that you do not know of any wills or codicils other than those referred to in the form. You are called the deponent since the Scottish legal term for swearing to a statement is deponing.

You take the will and the form (A-3 or B-4) completed (apart from the details relating to the oath on page 2) to a person entitled to administer oaths. Notaries public (most solicitors are notaries), justices of the peace, judges and certain officials in the sheriff court can take oaths from executors. (Solicitors charge about £20.) Where the deceased left a holograph will (a will entirely in his or her own handwriting and not witnessed) made before 1 August 1995, you must also produce sworn statements by two people that the will is genuine.

The form and other documents are signed by you and the person administering the oath and then the details of the taking of the oath are filled in on page 2.

Paying inheritance tax

Any tax due by the executors must be paid before confirmation can be applied for. You send off the completed Form A-3 (there should be no tax payable by executors in B-4 estates) together with a cheque payable to the Inland Revenue, to the Capital Taxes Office (see above). If you have difficulty working out how much is due they will help you. At this stage, the amount payable is only provisional as the value of some items may be altered or additional items of estate may come to light. After a short interval, the Capital Taxes Office will send you back the form stamped on the last page to show that tax has been paid.

Lodging the form

The final step is to lodge (usually by post but you can do it personally) the form with the sheriff court for the place where the deceased was domiciled at the time of his death. If you are in any doubt which one that is, your local sheriff court will help you. You must also lodge the will and pay the fee for *confirmation. For estates not exceeding £50,000 the fee is £70; for estates larger than £50,000 the fee is £100.*

After a week or so, if everything is in order, the confirmation will be sent to you by post. At or about the same time the will is returned, the court keeping a copy for its records. The confirmation is a photocopy of parts of the form you lodged showing details of the deceased, the executors and all the items of the estate in the United Kingdom together with a page in which the sheriff principal 'in Her Majesty's name and authority approves of and confirms' the named executor(s) and 'gives and commits to the said executor(s) full power' in relation to the estate.

You will need to show the confirmation to all those holding property which belonged to the deceased as evidence of your right to demand and receive it. (That is why it is important that all the items in the estate were listed; if not, you may have to go back to the court to get confirmation for excluded items.) For an estate with many items, to speed things up, you can get certificates of confirmation for individual items of estate. These cost £3 each if ordered when you apply for confirmation. (You have to speci-fy clearly the individual items for which certificates are required, for example the life policy, the house, the bank account, or the British Telecom shares, etc.) You can then send out the appropriate certificate of confirmation to each of the various bodies simultaneously.

Additional step if there is no will: appointment of executors

Where the deceased died without a will, one of his or her relatives has to be appointed executor by the court. A surviving widow(er) who inherits the whole estate by prior rights is entitled to be appointed sole executor. Even where other members of the family get a share of the estate, the widow(er) is normally made an executor, although the others can be appointed in addition. Where no widow(er) is left, the children (or some of them) are appointed. Adult children can also be appointed if the widow(er) is not able to take on the job of being executor. Some courts require proof of the widow(er)'s incapacity; others require the widow(er) to renounce all rights to the estate before children can be appointed in place of the widow(er), if the children are not entitled to any share of the estate. Failing the widow(er) and children, a relative who inherits all or part of the estate will be appointed.

The relative proposing to act as executor applies to the sheriff court for the place where the deceased was domiciled at the time of his death. The application has to be made by petition and there is no printed form for lay executors to complete. It is probably best to ask a solicitor to prepare the petition (the cost including court fees will amount to about £120). The petition is normally granted within a few days unless an objection has been lodged.

Additional step if there is no will: bond of caution

If you are an executor appointed by the court, you are required to provide a guarantee that you will carry out your duties as executor properly before confirmation will be issued to you. This guarantee is called a bond of caution (pronounced 'kayshun').

Losses caused by your negligence or fraud are made good by the cautioner in the first instance, but the cautioner will then attempt to recover from you the money paid. Usually an insurance company will act as cautioner, the premium being about £1.50 per £1,000 value of the estate. Insurance companies are not very keen to act as cautioners to executors who are going to administer the estate without professional assistance unless the estate is small and its administration straightforward. You may have to use a solicitor simply because you cannot obtain caution from an insurance company. Instead of an insurance company, you can have an individual as a cautioner, but the court has to be satisfied that the individual is rich enough to pay up if called on to do so.

You do not have to provide a bond of caution if you are the deceased's widow(er) and you inherit the whole estate by virtue of your prior rights.

Small estates

To reduce the expense of obtaining confirmation, there are special procedures for small estates. An estate is small if its gross value (the value of all the assets without any deduction being made for debts) does not exceed £17,000. For a small estate:

- *where there is no will, you do not have to petition the court for appointment of an executor*
- *no inheritance tax will be payable (unless the deceased made a large number of chargeable lifetime gifts)*
- *the necessary forms will be completed for you by the staff at the sheriff court.*

You can apply to any convenient sheriff court. If a personal visit could be inconvenient, you may apply by post to the sheriff court for the place in which the deceased was domiciled at the time of his death. If you are housebound, you will have to ask a person entitled to administer oaths (such as a justice of the peace) to call at the house, so that you can swear your oath as to the accuracy of the information in the form.

The small estates procedure for cases where there is a will is slightly different from those where no will was left.

Where there is a will

You need to take (or send) to the sheriff court a list of all the items in the estate with their values, a list of all the debts (including the funeral account), a note of the deceased's full name and address, date of birth and date and place of death, and the will. The sheriff clerk will then prepare Form B-3, for you to sign then and there, or will ask you to return in a few days' time. The fee for confirmation is payable on signing the form. No fee is charged if the estate does not exceed £5,000 in value. The fee is £70 for estates over £5,000 but not exceeding £17,000.

A few days after you have signed the form, the confirmation will be sent to you by post. The will is returned to you, the court keeping a copy for its records.

Where there is no will

Since there is no executor appointed by will, the court has to appoint one (see page 199 for who may be appointed). The person proposing to act as executor does not have to petition the court: it is part of the application for confirmation where the estate is small. The prospective executor takes (or sends) a list of all the items in the estate with their values, a list of all the debts, and a note of the deceased's full name and address, date of birth and place of death.

The sheriff clerk of the court dealing with your application will complete Form B-3 from the information you have supplied. You will be asked to return in a few days' time together with two witnesses who can swear to your identity and relationship to the deceased. At this stage you have to pay a fee, as above, unless the estate is below £5,000 in value.

Before confirmation will be issued to you, you will have to lodge a bond of caution (see opposite). This requirement is waived if you are the deceased's widow(er) and you inherit the whole estate by virtue of your prior rights. The confirmation will be posted to you a few days later.

Debts and legal rights

One of your main duties as executor is to pay the deceased's debts. These fall into three categories.

First come secured debts. Examples are a building society loan where the building society has a security over the deceased's home or an overdraft for which the bank holds a life policy as security. You have to pay secured debts, otherwise the creditor will sell the property held as security and take payment out of the money realised.

Next come privileged debts. They include medical and funeral expenses, the cost of obtaining confirmation, value added tax (but not any other tax) due by the deceased, and the unpaid wages of any employee of the deceased up to a set maximum per employee. You can pay privileged debts as soon as you have money to do so, unless the deceased was bankrupt or his or her estate is insolvent.

Finally, there are ordinary debts. All ordinary creditors who claim within six months of the deceased's death are entitled to equal treatment. This means you cannot be compelled to pay ordinary debts or distribute any items from the estate until the six-month period has elapsed. You should use your common sense here. If the estate has plenty of assets and you have no suspicion that there might be large unpaid debts, you can pay creditors, particularly small tradesmen, as soon as you have the money. Similarly, small bequests (golf clubs or a picture, for example) can safely be made over once confirmation has been obtained.

You must not forget about legal rights if the deceased left a widow(er), children, including adopted children and children born outwith marriage, or other descendants. You should write to every person who could claim, telling them how much their legal rights are worth and suggesting they take legal advice before deciding whether to claim or renounce.

Children present a problem. If they are under 16 they cannot legally decide whether to renounce or claim, and the widow(er) cannot renounce on their behalf as guardian, since he or she will have a conflicting interest. Children aged 16 and 17 can renounce but the court should be asked to ratify this. Without ratification children can apply to the court when they have grown up if they feel they renounced wrongly. Where the legal rights are under £5,000 the executors may hand over the money to the *surviving parent (or guardian) who should invest it for the children, or the executors may open a building society account or buy National Savings certificates in the child's name and hand over the passbook or certificates to the parent. A parent (or guardian) who misappropriates the money may be sued for its return. For sums over £20,000 the executors should contact the Accountant of Court at Parliament House.* After considering the circumstances the Accountant will decide how the money is to be best managed. The options are: a court–appointed manager (for large sums only), the Accountant to be manager, or the parent (or guardian) to be manager but supervised by the Accountant. The executors may, but need not, contact the Accountant for sums between £5,000 and £20,000.*

Finding unknown creditors

There is no official procedure in Scotland for advertising for creditors. Executors are protected against the emergence of unknown creditors in a different way.

After six months from the date of death, executors are entitled to pay all known creditors and distribute the balance of the estate to the beneficiaries. Creditors who claim later are paid if the executors still have estate in their hands. Executors who have no estate left do not have to pay later creditors out of their own pockets unless they should, in the circumstances, have known of the existence of further creditors. Occasionally advertising will be a sensible way of discovering unknown creditors. But local newspapers or trade journals (if the deceased was in business) would be used rather than the Edinburgh Gazette.

Transfer of the house

The executor is not involved in transferring the house of the person who died if the title contained a survivorship destination. The deceased's share of the house is automatically transferred to the surviving co-owner.

In other cases, you can transfer the house by a simple document called a docket. This may be used only if the transferee – the person to whom you are transferring the house – is a beneficiary under the will or the intestacy rules or a person claiming legal rights. Transfer to other categories of person, a purchaser for example, requires a document called a disposition. Dispositions are best prepared by solicitors.

The docket consists of a form written or typed on the back of the confirmation or, better, the certificate of confirmation relating to the house. Use of a certificate avoids parting with the confirmation which you may need to retain for other purposes. The same form of docket is used whether the title to the house is registered in the Sasine Register or the Land Register for Scotland. The docket is as follows:

I *(executor's full name)*, being by virtue of the within certificate of confirmation the executor on the estate of *(the deceased's full name)* so far as specified in the confirmation hereby nominate *(the transferee's full name and address)* as the person entitled
* * [in [part] satisfaction of his/her claim to prior rights, as a surviving spouse, on the death of the deceased]; or
* * [in [part] satisfaction of his/her claim to legal right on the death of the deceased]; or
* * [in [part] satisfaction of his/her share of the estate]; or
* * [in [part] implement of the will of the deceased dated *(insert date of will)*]

to the following item of estate, that is to say *(the postal address of the house)* being number *(item number of house in the inventory of estate)* of the items of estate specified in the said confirmation.

In witness whereof I have signed this docket at *(place of signing)* on *(date of signing)* before the following witness *(witness's full name and address)*.

Witness's signature   Executor's signature

You should select the appropriate reason from the four options given in the form above. You sign the docket before a witness who signs as well and then you complete the details of the signing and the document is ready to be handed to the transferee.

Even if you yourself are the transferee, you will still have to do a docket transferring the house from yourself as an executor to yourself as an individual.

Where the house is registered in the Land Register for Scotland, the transferee can have it put in his or her name simply by applying to the Keeper at Meadowbank House,* and enclosing the certificate of confirmation and docket. In the case of unregistered land, a solicitor would have to prepare a 'Notice of Title' which would then be recorded in the Sasine Register. Many transferees do not bother with a Notice of Title. When *they come to sell the house eventually, they can use the docket as evidence of their right to the house.*

The docket is a very important document and may be difficult or impossible to replace if lost. It is usual to register it in the Books of Council and Session, a national register of deeds kept at the Registers of Scotland, Meadowbank House.* (Any deed can be registered there: the original document is retained, and you will receive a certified copy of it.)

Discharge of building society loan

Where the house is registered in the Land Register for Scotland the procedure to discharge a building society loan is similar to that described for England and Wales. For unregistered land, the building society will send you a document called a discharge which you should record in the Sasine Register, which is situated at Meadowbank House.*

Interest on legacies

Interest can be claimed on a legacy if the executor has delayed unreasonably in paying it. There is no fixed rate; it depends on what the estate has on average been earning.

Legacies to children under 16

What should happen depends on the value of the legacy. For a legacy under £5,000 the executors may pay it to the parents (or guardians) of the child to invest on the child's behalf. If the legacy is large (over £20,000) the executors must contact the Accountant of Court.* After considering the circumstances the Accountant will decide how the money is to be best managed. The options are: a court–appointed manager (for large sums only), the Accountant to be manager, or the parents (or guardians) to be manager but supervised by the Accountant. For sums between £5,000 and £20,000 the executors may, but need not, contact the Accountant.

CHAPTER 9

DISTRIBUTION ON INTESTACY IN SCOTLAND

There is no difference between executors-nominate (those appointed by the will) and executors-dative (those appointed by the court) in the way they collect in and administer the estate. But when it comes to distributing the estate, executors-nominate do so in accordance with the will, while executors-dative have to follow the intestacy rules in the Succession (Scotland) Act 1964.

Where the deceased died without a will, one of his or her relatives has to be appointed executor by the court. A surviving widow(er) who inherits the whole estate by prior rights is entitled to be appointed sole executor. Even where other members of the family get a share of the estate, the widow(er) is normally made an executor, although the others can be appointed in addition. Where no widow(er) is left, the children (or some of them) are appointed. Children can also be appointed if the widow(er) does not feel able to take on the job of being executor. Such an appointment requires the widow(er)'s consent, however, if the children are not entitled to any share of the estate. Failing the widow(er) and children, the relative or relatives who inherit all or part of the estate will be appointed.

A person can inherit from any relative whether or not the link between them involves births outwith marriage. A divorced person cannot inherit from the ex-spouse under the rules of intestacy. A husband judicially separated from his wife does not inherit any of her intestate estate which she acquires after separation. There is no equivalent rule barring a separated wife inheriting. Cohabitants have no rights on intestacy to the estates of their deceased partners. A person who is disappointed with what (if anything) he or she receives under the intestacy rules cannot apply to the court for a suitable provision. The Inheritance (Provision for Family and Dependants) Act 1975 does not apply in Scotland.

The division of the net estate where the deceased died without leaving a will depends on the size of the estate, the nature of the assets and debts and what relatives survive. This is much more complex where there is a widow(er) because of prior and legal rights. The more straightforward case of a single or widowed person's estate is dealt with first.

Deceased leaves no widow(er)

Where the deceased dies without leaving a widow(er) the estate passes to the surviving relatives in the following order: descendants (children, grandchildren, etc.); brothers, sisters (and their descendants) and parents; uncles and aunts (and their descendants); grandparents; great-uncles and aunts (and their descendants); great-grandparents and so on until some relative is found to inherit.

Children

The children share the estate equally between them. Children of a child who died before the deceased take what would have been that child's share. If all the children are dead, the grandchildren share the estate equally among themselves, the descendants of a deceased grandchild taking their dead parent's share.

Children include adopted children, but not stepchildren.

Brothers, sisters and parents

Where the deceased left no surviving parents, his brothers and sisters share the whole estate. The descendants of a dead brother or sister inherit what would have been their father's or mother's share. Half-brothers and half-sisters get a share only if there are no full brothers or sisters or their descendants. A child who has been jointly adopted by a couple is treated as a full brother or sister of any other child they adopt or of any child of their marriage.

Where there are no brothers or sisters or their descendants surviving, the parents inherit the estate equally between them. If only one parent survives, he or she inherits the entire estate.

207

Where there are both brothers, sisters or their descendants and a parent or parents left, the estate is divided into two. Each half is further divided as described above.

Uncles and aunts

Next come brothers and sisters of the deceased's parents – his or her uncles and aunts. Children of an uncle or aunt who died before the deceased (the deceased's cousins) share equally between them the share their parent would have inherited had he or she survived. The same rule applies to the deceased's uncles' and aunts' remoter descendants – first cousins once removed, twice removed and so on.

Grandparents

Next in line are the deceased's grandparents. They share the estate between them or, if there is only one alive, he or she inherits the entire estate.

Remoter relatives

After grandparents come great-uncles and great-aunts or their descendants (namely second cousins, second cousins once removed, etc.). Children of a dead relative who would have inherited take the share their parent would have taken had he or she survived the deceased. If there are still no surviving relatives, the search continues back one generation at a time until hopefully someone is found to inherit.

The Crown

Where the deceased died without any surviving relatives being traced, the estate goes to the Crown. After debts and funeral expenses have been paid, the estate is handed over to the Queen's and Lord Treasurer's Remembrancer. This official advertises for claimants in local newspapers. If no relative claims the estate after advertisement, the Crown may be prepared to make gifts from the estate to people who have a moral but no legal claim to the estate, such as a co-habiting partner or a neighbour who did a lot for the deceased without payment.

Deceased leaves a widow(er)

Briefly the law provides first for the widow(er) who has prior rights to part or all of the estate. Next come the 'legal rights' of the widow(er) and any children. The remainder of the estate (if any) is taken by the nearest relatives.

Prior rights

These comprise a right to the house, a right to its furnishings and a right to a cash sum.

The house

The widow(er) is entitled to the house owned by the deceased provided it is situated in Scotland, he or she was ordinarily resident in the house at the date of the deceased's death, and that it is not worth more than £110,000. Where the deceased owned only a share of the house, the widow(er) gets that share provided the share is worth less than £110,000 and the other conditions are satisfied.

The widow(er) will get £110,000 instead of the house or share of the house if it or the share is worth more than £110,000. If the house is part of a larger property run as a business and it would be disadvantageous to split off the house, the widow(er) gets the value (up to £110,000) instead of the house. This situation could arise with a farmhouse.

Where the house has a loan secured over it, the widow(er) receives only the net value – the value of the house less the outstanding balance of the loan. This is so even if the deceased had a life policy to pay off the loan on death.

The furnishings

The widow(er) is entitled to up to £20,000 of furnishings which were owned by the deceased. Cars, jewellery and money do not count as furnishings. The furnishings need not be situated in a home owned by the deceased. The house may have been rented or belong to the widow(er) already, for example. Where the furnishings are worth more than £20,000, the widow(er) may select items to this value.

Cash sum

The widow(er) gets up to £50,000 if the deceased left no children or other descendants, but only up to £30,000 otherwise.

Prior rights are very valuable. The widow(er) usually ends up inheriting the entire estate unless it is large. Large intestate estates, however, are uncommon.

Legal rights

These come into play after prior rights have been taken. The widow(er) is entitled to one-third of the remaining net moveable estate (estate other than land and buildings) if there are surviving children. The children share another one-third between them. If there are no surviving children or other descendants, the widow(er)'s fraction is increased to one half.

The figure for the remaining net moveable estate needed for working out legal rights can be very complicated to calculate. Debts and liabilities of the estate must be set against either land and buildings (heritable estate) or the moveable estate. A loan secured over the house is a debt against the heritable estate, the funeral account and ordinary bills are debts against the moveable estate, while inheritance tax and the expenses of administration are apportioned between the heritable estate and the moveable estate depending on the relative values of each in the total estate. Finally, where the deceased owned heritable estate apart from the house, the prior right cash sum of £50,000 or £30,000 is treated as having been taken partly from the other heritable estate and partly from the moveable estate.

Children normally share the money representing their legal rights equally between them. Where one of the children dies before the deceased, leaving children, these children – the deceased's grandchildren – share the dead child's share. Where all the children have died, all the grandchildren share equally. A child who renounces his or her legal rights while the deceased was alive does not share, nor can his or her descendants. A child's share can also be affected if the deceased gave him or her a substantial marriage gift or money to set him or her up in life.

The remainder of the estate

The remainder of the estate, after prior and legal rights have been met, goes to the deceased's nearest relatives. The order is children, grandchildren and remoter descendants, then brothers, sisters (or their descendants) and parents. The rules for division between these relatives are the same as where the deceased left no widow(er).

If the deceased leaves no surviving relatives in the above categories, the widow(er) inherits the entire estate.

CHAPTER 10

WILLS AND PROBATE IN NORTHERN IRELAND

The law on wills and probate in Northern Ireland is similar to that in England and Wales. Indeed the law relating to wills is now almost identical following the introduction of new legislation on 1 January 1995. This new legislation generally applies to wills made both before and after this date, regardless of when the testator died.

One major difference between England and Northern Ireland has been created by the new legislation. In Northern Ireland a married minor or minors who have been married can now make a valid will provided the will is actually signed after 1 January 1995. It is not possible for a married minor in England to make a valid will.

After someone dies and probate has been obtained, anyone can apply to see it or obtain a copy of it at the Probate Office, Royal Courts of Justice.* If it is more than five years since the grant was obtained then application should be made to the Public Records Office of Northern Ireland.*

Public Trustee (page 35)

The Public Trustee service is not available in Northern Ireland.

Husband and wife (page 41)

In Northern Ireland the common law presumption of simultaneous deaths in cases where it is not certain who died first still applies.

Solicitors' fees (pages 82–3)

There is no recommended scale of fees for solicitors. However, the profession in Northern Ireland tends to follow these guidelines:

- *on the first £10,000 of the gross value of the estate*   2½%
- *on the next £20,000 of the gross value of the estate*   2%
- *on the next £220,000 of the gross value of the estate*   1½%

Where the gross value of the estate includes the principal private dwelling house this is normally reduced in value by 50% for the purpose of calculating fees. In addition fees are charged in respect of the time spent by various members of staff in the solicitor's office.

Executor not wishing to act (page 92)

It is possible for a person named as an executor in a will to appoint an attorney only if the executor resides outside Northern Ireland or is incapable of managing his own affairs and a controller has been appointed by the Office of Care and Protection.

The value of the holding (pages 105–8)

While many people living in Northern Ireland hold government stock registered on the Bank of England Register, there is also a Bank of Ireland register maintained at the Bank of Ireland (Registration Department).* The relevant stock certificate or interest counterfoil will indicate whether the stock is registered on the Bank of England or the Bank of Ireland register. A third register is operated by the Department for National Savings, Bonds and Stock Office.*

Advertising for creditors (page 118–19)

The special procedure for formally advertising for creditors in Northern Ireland requires an advertisement in the Belfast Gazette *and an advertisement twice in each of two papers circulating in the area in which the deceased died.*

Applying for probate forms (page 119)

Personal applications should be made to the Personal Application Department, Probate and Matrimonial Office, Royal Courts of Justice* or the District Probate Registry.* If the deceased had a fixed place of abode within the counties of Fermanagh, Londonderry or Tyrone the application may be made to either of these addresses but if the deceased resided outside these counties the application must be made to the Belfast office.

The fees in all applications are based on the net value of the estate. They are as follows:

- net estate under £10,000   nil
- net estate £10,000–£25,000   £60
- net estate between £25,000–£40,000   £120
- net estate between £40,000–£70,000   £220
- net estate between £70,000–£100,000   £320
- net estate between £100,000–£200,000   £400

and £65 for each additional £100,000 thereafter.

The additional fee paid in a personal application is £6 for each £1,000 of the net estate or part thereof.

Other arrangements for IHT money (page 121)

The cheque for the inheritance tax should be made out to 'Inland Revenue' while the cheque for the Probate Office fees should be made out to 'The Supreme Court Fees Account'.

Form PA1 (pages 127–8)

In Northern Ireland it is not yet necessary to serve a notice on an executor who is not acting and who has not renounced. Therefore it is possible for one executor to obtain probate of a will without another executor even being aware that he is an executor.

Transfer of the house (pages 161–8)

In Northern Ireland property is either registered or unregistered as in England, although land law legislation in Northern Ireland is very different from that in England and Wales.

Registered property (pages 162–5)

In the case of registered land the executors or the administrators complete an assent (Form 32). A specimen form appears in Appendix I.

The completed Form 32 is then sent to the Land Registry* together with the land certificate, the original grant of probate or letters of administration and Form 100. A specimen Form 100 appears in Appendix II. Both forms

32 and 100 are available from the Land Registry. The fee charged by the Land Registry is £25 if the value of the property is less than £10,000 and £50 if the value of the property is over this level. If the property was subject to a mortgage the certificate of charge with the vacate (receipt) sealed by the bank or building society should be lodged at the same time together with an additional fee of £10 if the value of the charge exceeds £500 and £25 where the value of the charge exceeds £5,000. Cheques should be made payable to 'Land Registry of Northern Ireland'.

Unregistered property (pages 165–7)

Unregistered land is in fact registered in the Registry of Deeds. Although no particular form of words is required in order to vest property in a beneficiary the wording varies as to whether the title to the property is freehold, fee farm grant or leasehold and as to whether the property has been specifically bequeathed or forms part of the residue. It is best to consult a solicitor to prepare an assent for unregistered land. The solicitor will be able to arrange for a memorial of the assent to be registered in the Registry of Deeds for which the Registry charges a fee of £14. The memorial is an extract of the assent giving the date, names of the parties executing the deed, the address of the property and whether the property is freehold or leasehold. At present the memorial must be typed on memorial paper which is of a size which does not fit into modern typewriters.

Distribution on intestacy (Chapter 7)

The main difference between English and Northern Irish law is with regard to the rules on intestacy. In Northern Ireland no life interests are created on intestacy. Administrators must apply the intestacy rules laid down in the Administration of Estates Act (Northern Ireland) 1955. As in England the nearest relatives in a fixed order are entitled to apply for the grant and if the nearest relative does not wish to apply he can renounce his right to do so, in which case the next nearest becomes entitled to be the administrator.

The surviving spouse is primarily entitled to be the administrator. Where there is a surviving spouse, he or she is always entitled to the personal effects, no matter how great their value. If there is a child the surviving spouse is entitled to the first £125,000 net of the estate together with interest thereon at 6% from the date of death to the date of payment and to one-half of the residue after payment of all debts and administration expenses. The remaining half share of the residue passes to the child either absolutely if the child is over 18 or in trust until the child becomes 18.

If there are two or more children the surviving spouse receives one-third of the residue (instead of one-half where there is only one child) while the remaining children divide the two-thirds share of the residue between them. This applies no matter how many children there may be.

If there is no surviving spouse the entire estate is divided equally between the children and if any child has died before the intestate then any children of the deceased child divide their parent's share between them. As in England no distinction is made between natural or adopted children.

Where someone dies intestate without children but one or both parents of the intestate are still alive, then the surviving spouse (if any) receives the first £200,000 of the estate plus interest thereon at 6% per annum from the date of death until payment together with one-half of the residue. The other half of the residue passes to the parents of the intestate equally or, if only one parent is still alive, to that parent in its entirety. If there is no surviving spouse, the parents will inherit the entire estate equally or if only one parent survives, then that parent will inherit the entire estate.

Where someone dies without children and without parents but with brothers or sisters or children of predeceased brothers and sisters, then the surviving spouse (if any) takes the first £200,000 plus interest thereon at 6% from the date of death to the date of payment and one-half of the residue. The other half of the residue is divided between the surviving brothers and sisters. The children of a predeceased brother or sister divide their parent's share equally between them. It should be noted that the brothers and sisters of the surviving spouse do not share in this distribution – only the actual brothers and sisters of the intestate do. If there is no surviving spouse, then the entirety is divided between the brothers and sisters with the issue of any predeceased brother or sister taking their parent's share.

Another major difference between English and Northern Irish law is that in Northern Ireland if there are no issue, parents, siblings, grandparents or uncles or aunts or their issue, the pecking order to determine the next-of-kin continues through great-grandparents, grand-uncles and grand-aunts, great-great-grandparents, great-grand-uncles and great-grand-aunts and children of grand-uncles and grand-aunts, great-great-

great-grandparents, second cousins (that is, children of the children of grand-uncles and grand-aunts or the children of great-grand-uncles and great-grand-aunts) to other next-of-kin of the nearest degree. As the distribution is exceedingly wide it is sensible to consult a solicitor if any of these categories apply.

The following examples relate to those given in Chapter 7, but assume that the deceased had died while domiciled in Northern Ireland.

Example A

Deceased's family
Wife and three children.

Net estate
Personal effects (that is, strictly, 'personal chattels', including car unless it was used for business purposes – furniture, clothing, jewellery and all goods and chattels) and £9,500 (in savings bank, savings certificates). They lived in rented accommodation.

Division of estate under intestacy rules
All to wife.

Explanation
The entire estate will pass to the wife, as the surviving spouse takes the personal effects no matter how great their value and the first £125,000 of the rest of the net estate.

Example B

Deceased's family
Wife and three adult children.

Net estate
Personal effects and £185,000 including investments and value of house which was owned solely by the deceased husband.

Division of estate under intestacy rules
(1) wife gets:
  (a) personal effects
  (b) £125,000 plus interest thereon at 6% per annum from the date of death until payment
  (c) £20,000 absolutely
(2) the three children get £40,000 divided between them equally i.e. £13,333.33 each.

Explanation
The intestacy rules give the widow all the personal effects, £125,000 (plus interest at 6% from the date of death to the date of payment) and one-third of the remainder. They give the remaining two-thirds to the children equally.

If one of the children had died before the father, leaving any children, then those grandchildren of the deceased would have shared their parent's portion of their grandfather's estate. As in England it makes no difference if the widow is not the mother of some or all of the children.

Example C

Deceased's family
Wife and four children; two of them (A and B) are over 18 years old at the deceased's death and two of them (C and D) are younger than 18.

Net estate
Personal effects and £149,000 made up of £129,000 of investments, and half the value of the house worth £40,000 which was owned as tenants-in-common in equal shares by husband and wife.

Division of estate under intestacy rules
(1) wife gets:
  (a) personal effects
  (b) £125,000 plus interest thereon at 6% per annum from date of death until payment
  (c) £8,000 absolutely

(2) the four children receive £16,000 between them, i.e. £4,000 each.

Explanation
The explanation for example C is similar to that for example B. As the wife already owns half the house, then only half of the value of the house will be distributed because that is all that the deceased owned. The widow may take the other half-share in the house as part of her legacy of £125,000. The administrator will invest the money for the two minor children until they respectively become 18. Therefore at 18 the two minor children should receive more than £4,000 as the value of the investment should have increased even though some of the income may have been applied for their maintenance before they become 18.

Example D

The situation is as for example C, but the house was owned by husband and wife as joint tenants. Therefore, regardless of the intestacy rules, the wife acquires the rest of the house automatically and becomes the sole owner. The intestacy rules operate only on the rest of the estate so the wife gets:

(a) personal effects
(b) £125,000 plus interest thereon at 6% per annum from date of death until payment
(b) £1,333.33 absolutely.

The children divide £2,666.67 between them (i.e. they each receive £666.66 absolutely). Again there is no life interest under the intestacy rules in Northern Ireland and where there is more than one child the surviving spouse receives one-third of the residue while two-thirds of the residue is divided between the children.

Examples E-J will have the same results in Northern Ireland as in England.

Example K

Deceased's family
Five second cousins (relatives who have the same great-grand-parents as the deceased).

Net estate
£10,000

Division of estate under intestacy rules
Each second cousin will receive £2,000.

Explanation
Unlike in England, second cousins inherit and where they are all related in the same degree they inherit equally.

The legislation concerning possible claims by next of kin is contained in the Inheritance (Provision for Family and Dependants) (Northern Ireland) Order 1977. The legislation is similar to the 1975 English Act. Anyone considering making a claim should consult a solicitor.

LAND REGISTRY ASSENT FORM

Instructions for completion

(1) General

Complete all relevant panels and schedules. If the space is insufficient continuation sheet(s) (size A4) should be securely attached. Each continuation sheet must be headed with the appropriate folio number(s) and county, and reference to the panel or schedule to which it relates. A cross-reference note should also be included in the panel or schedule (e.g. 'continued on attached sheet').

(2) The deceased

Insert appropriate details and have the Certificate of Identity on page 4 completed.

(3) The personal representatives

Insert full name(s) and address(es) and description(s). If the details differ from those in the Grant include explanatory words (*e.g. 'formerly of/known as ...'*). If a name has changed since the Grant, furnish appropriate evidence.

(4) Settlements

(i)   The entire panel should be deleted if a settlement has not been created.

(ii)   The reference to trustees may be deleted if there are no trustees of the settlement for the purpose of the Settled Land Acts.

(5) The property

(i)   Identify the land or estate the subject of the Assent. If all the land in a folio is being vested in the Assentee(s), this must be made clear.

(ii)   If part only of the land in a folio is being vested, insert a description referring to colours on an attached map.

(iii)   The part being vested should be defined on an extract from the latest available OS plan drawn to the largest published scale. (In cases of a very small plot or for an area of complex OS detail the location map must be supplemented by a larger-scale plan.)

(iv)   All maps/plans must be securely fastened to the Assent.

(v)   If the Assent deals with two or more separate pieces of land it may be necessary to number the entries in this column.

(6) The assentee

(i)   Enter the full name(s), postal address(es) in the UK for service of notices and descriptions(s) of the Assentee(s) for entry in the register.

(ii)   If an assentee is an existing owner of an estate in the land, or a minor, that fact must be stated.

(7) Assentees' share

If the Assent is to two or more persons who are to hold as tenants in common, that fact must be stated and the precise fractional shares which pass to each person must also be stated (*e.g. if the Assent is of an undivided half-share to two tenants in common who take equally, the appropriate entry in the 'share' column opposite each person would be 'one-quarter' **not** 'one-half' or 'equal'*). If no shares are specified any co-assentees will be taken to be joint tenants *inter se*.

(8) Class of ownership

State whether the Assentee is to be registered as 'FULL OWNER' or (where a settlement has been created) as 'LIMITED OWNER' of the land.

(9) The burdens

(i)   Give precise details of the burden.

(ii)   Identify which folio or part of a folio and, where necessary, whose estate or interest therein is subject to the burden. (Where the burden does not affect all the Land in this Assent make this clear – *e.g. 'affecting only the land in entry 1 of the First Schedule/the land shown coloured ... on the attached map/the dwelling house on the land in Folio ...'*).

(iii)   If a burden is a charge for payment of money identify it as such and state whether interest is payable.

(iv)   If two or more burdens are to be registered, their priority *inter se* should be clarified.

(10) Person entitled to burden

Where the burden is a charge or right of residence, maintenance or support, state the name, address in the UK for the service of notices and description of any person entitled to the benefit of the burden.

(11) Execution

Unless witnessed by a solicitor the Assent must be witnessed by two people neither of whom is a party to the Assent. Witnesses must subscribe their names, addresses and descriptions.

(12) Certificate of identity

(i)   The relevant details should be completed and the certificate should be signed by the solicitor handling the deceased's estate or, if none, by an independent person having knowledge of the facts.

(ii)   Add any other certificate of identity which may be necessary to prove that the personal representative is entitled to make the Assent.

LAND REGISTRY   **FORM 32**

ASSENT BY PERSONAL REPRESENTATIVE

COMPLETE PANELS AS PER ATTACHED INSTRUCTIONS

Note 1

County: XXX	Date: 1 November 1997
All Folio(s) affected:	**Registered Owner(s):**
FOLIO NO. YYY	OONAGH MARY O'BRIEN

Note 2

Deceased Registered Owner: OONAGH MARY O'BRIEN
who died on: 12 MAY 1997

Note 3

The Personal Representative(s) of the said deceased:
1. Patricia Helen Partridge, 3 Lower Street, Belfast – Teacher 2. Norman Bruce Martin, 28 Paul Avenue, Belfast – Radiographer

I/We the above named personal representative(s), for the purpose of administering the estate of the deceased Registered Owner, assent to the vesting of the property described in the First Schedule in the Assentee(s) as set out in the said Schedule and request registration accordingly, subject as appears in the folio(s) and also subject to registration of the burden(s)(if any) set out in the Second Schedule.

Note 4

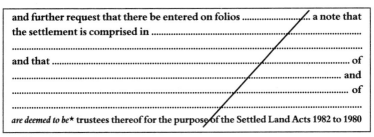

and further request that there be entered on folios ..../... a note that the settlement is comprised in ....
....
and that .... of
.... **and**
.... **of**
....
are deemed to be * **trustees thereof for the purpose of the Settled Land Acts 1982 to 1980**

* *delete if inappropriate*

THE FIRST SCHEDULE

The Property (Note 5)	The Assentee(s) (Note 6)	Assentees' Share (Note7)	Class of ownership (Note 8)
All the land in Folio YYY County XXX	Peter Morris Eltham Park House Beech Avenue Marbleton Co. Antrim	All	Fee Simple

THE SECOND SCHEDULE

Burdens (Note 9)	Person(s) entitled to benefit of burden (Note 10)
None	None

Note 11

SIGNED SEALED AND DELIVERED
by the said PATRICIA HELEN PARTRIDGE
in the presence of:

SIGNED SEALED AND DELIVERED
by the said NORMAN BRUCE MARTIN
in presence of:

Certificate of Identity – Note 12

I NORMAN BRUCE MARTIN

of 28 Paul Avenue, Belfast

hereby certify that OONAGH MARY O'BRIEN

named in a Grant of Probate of the Will

issued on 9 July 1995 **is one and the same person as** OONAGH MARY
O'BRIEN **the registered owner of the within mentioned folio(s)**

Dated this   **day of**   **199**

Signed ....

Land Registry of Northern Ireland

Form 100

Application for Registration

Please complete the white boxes on pages 1 & 2 using typescript or BLOCK LETTERS. No covering letter is necessary.

Fee Impression

1. County : XXX		Pending Applications
Folio(s) affected	Registered owners	
YYY	OONAGH MARY O'BRIEN	

If insufficient space continue on a separate sheet and enter 'See list'.

2. Clients.

PATRICIA HELEN PARTRIDGE AND NORMAN BRUCE MARTIN

3. Fees and Priority

Describe each dealing concisely and indicate whether it affects the *WHOLE* or *PART* of the Folio.

Include request for a land certificate and / or a copy map if required (See also panel 7).

Include request for a Certificate of Charge where required.

Full fees are payable on delivery of application.

A separate statement of value is required if 'Value' panel is not completed.

List applications in priority order	Value £	Fees Paid £	(Official use only) Details of over/under payment
RELEASE OF CHARGE	25,000	25.00	
ASSENT	125,000	50.00	

I / We enclose a crossed cheque / postal order payable to Land Registry, DOE (NI) for   Total | £ 75.00 | Excess refunded

FDC3.93 JK1.94

4. Applicants
Name and address of person or firm lodging this application to whom any queries should be sent and to whom documents should be returned unless any special directions are given in panel 5.

Queries to be sent to and documents returned to	
NORMAN BRUCE MARTIN	
28 PAUL AVENUE	
BELFAST	Postcode
Tel no. & code	Ref.

5. Special directions
Complete where any document is to be returned to a person or firm not mentioned in panel 4.

Description of document and addressee	
NONE	
	Postcode
Tel. no. & code	Ref.

6. Change of address
This panel may be completed if the address of any person named (or to be named) on the folio is to be updated.

Please update the address of	
to read : NOT APPLICABLE	
	Postcode

7. Requisition for New Land Certificate and/or copy map
NB Panel 3 must also be completed

Note : where application is for a copy map, indicate the appropriate Folio *and* type of map.

As solicitor(s) for [   ]

I / We apply for the following *(tick appropriate boxes)*

New Land Certificate *(if required)* ☐

Copy map	Certified ☐	New Folio	Folio No(s) ....
	Uncertified ☐	☐	☐ ....

8. Documents lodged - list all documents lodged *(attach continuation sheet, if required)*

Date	Document	Parties	Checked & ack.
–	FOLIO YYY	LAND CERTIFICATE	
–	CERTIFICATE OF CHARGE	OONAGH MARY O'BRIEN TO BUILDING SOCIETY	
9 JULY 1995	PROBATE	OONAGH MARY O'BRIEN DECEASED	
			Date

9. Checklist

a.	Have you enclosed the appropriate fee and signed the cheque?	☐	d. Where the application refers to a map, is map lodged?	☐
b.	Have all deeds been executed dated & witnessed?	☐	e. Have all necessary Land Certificates and Certificates of Charge been lodged? If not, have you lodged a request for an order for their production?	☐
c.	Have deeds been presented to the Stamp Office where required?	☐		

10. Declaration by applicant or solicitor

I / we certify that the information supplied is correct.	
Signature of applicant or solicitor	Date

ADDRESSES

Accountant of Court
2 Parliament Square
Edinburgh EH1 1RF
0131-225 2595

Age Concern England
Astral House
1268 London Road
Norbury
London SW16 4ER
0181-679 8000

**Bank of Ireland
(Registration)**
20 Callender Street
Belfast BT1 5BN
(01232) 315989

Capital Taxes Office
16 Picardy Place
Edinburgh EH1 3NB
0131-556 8511

Central Probate Registry
*(for anyone living in Northern
Ireland)*
Royal Courts of Justice
Chichester Street
Belfast BT1 3JF
(01232) 235111

**Department for National
Savings**
Boydstone Road
Glasgow G58 1SB
0141-649 4555
*(bank books, investment accounts
and ordinary accounts)*

**Department for National
Savings**
Millburngate House
Durham DH99 1NS
0191-386 4900
(NS certificates, deposit bonds)

**Department for National
Savings**
Bonds and Stock Office
Mythop Road
Marton
Blackpool FY3 9YP
(01253) 766151
*(premium bonds, income bonds, pen-
sioner's guaranteed bonds)*

District Probate Registry
*(for people living in Derry,
Fermanagh, Tyrone)*
Bishop Street
Londonderry BT48 6PY
(01504) 261832

FT Information Ltd
Fitzroy House
13–17 Epworth Street
London EC2A 4DL
0171-825 8000

HM Commissary Office
27 Chambers Street
Edinburgh EH1 1LB
0131-225 2525

HM Inspector of Anatomy
Department of Health
Wellington House
135–155 Waterloo Road
London SE1 8UG
0171-972 2000

HMSO
49 High Holborn
London WC1V 6HB
0171-873 0011

Land Registry (N.I.)
The Lincoln Buildings
27–45 Great Victoria Street
Belfast BT2 7SL
(01232) 251555

Meadowbank House
Registers of Scotland
153 London Road
Edinburgh EH8 7AU
0131-659 6111

Oyez Stationery
(The Solicitors' Law Stationery
Society)
Oyez House
7 Spa Road
London SE16 3QQ
0171-232 1000

**Principal Registry of the
Family Division**
South Wing
Somerset House
Strand
London WC2R 1LP
0171-936 6000

Royal Courts of Justice (N.I.)
Chichester Street
Belfast BT1 3JJ
(01232) 235111

Probate Registry
Somerset House
Strand
London WC2R 1LP
0171-936 6983

**Public Record Office of
Northern Ireland**
66 Balmoral Avenue
Belfast BT9 6NY
(01232) 255905

INDEX

abroad
    owning land 10, 136
    permanent home 14
absolute legacy 30, 38, 39
accountants as executors 33
Administration of Estates Act
    1925 7, 9, 180
Administration of Estates Act
    (Northern Ireland) 1955
    215
administrators 13, 32, 77, 80, 84–5
    of an intestate estate 180–1
    in Scotland 192
adopted children 181, 207
annuities 138
assent
    and registered property 163–4
    and unregistered property
    165–8
Assent or Appropriation (Form
    56) 163, 164, 165
    registration of 164
assets 156
    calculation of 94–109, 123–6
    collection of 146–53
    and form IHT 30: 152, 155–6
    held in trust 138
    probate form for (IHT 44)
    127, 129–31, 132–4, 136–9

attestation clauses 62, 63
aunts/uncles and intestacy 11,
    189, 191
    in Northern Ireland 216
    in Scotland 207, 208

bank accounts 79, 96–8, 130
    beneficiary's use of 147
    'either or survivor account'
    194
    executorship account 122,
    148, 171, 174
    and finance for IHT 121–3,
    170
    freezing 96, 123
    income tax on interest 168,
    169, 170
    joint accounts 97–8
    in Scotland 194
    overdrafts 89
banks
    as brokers 152
    as executors 34–5
    lodging wills with 64
    and share transfers 158–60
beneficiary
    as executor 50
    as witness to will 60, 74
    naming in will 37

predeceasing 40–2
  in Scotland 42, 72–3
residuary 38, 41
birthday gifts 24
bona vacantia 190
bond of caution (Scotland) 200,
  201
Books of Council and Session
  75, 205
brothers/sisters and intestacy 11,
  188
  in Northern Ireland 216
  in Scotland 207, 208
building society accounts 94,
  98–9, 130
  assets from 148, 154
  and finance for IHT 121
  see also mortgage debts

capital gains tax (CGT) 53,
  160–1
  on asset sale gains 168–9, 170
  exemptions from 152, 160–1
  on house sales 161
  and house valuation 100
  and lifetime gifts 16
  and share transfers 160–1
capital, life interest and 12
Capital Taxes Office 156
capital transfer tax (CTT) 15,
  25
cars 113, 114
  in Scotland 209
cash 130
certificates of confirmation 199,
  204
charge certificate 163, 165
charities, gifts to 18, 19, 38, 51
children
  adopted 181, 207
  adult children, bequests to
    56–8

and age of entitlement to
  inheritance 52
and disinheriting 40
  in Scotland 72
gifts to 18
and guardians 12, 35–6, 50,
  53, 66
illegitimate 181
infant children 33–4
and inheritance tax 21–2,
  57–8
and intestacy 10, 12, 187
legacy investments for 173
and lifetime gifts 16
and minority interests 82
and Northern Ireland laws of
  will making 215–16,
  218, 219
and Scottish laws of will
  making 72, 75–6,
  202–3, 205, 207
stepchildren 75, 207
and trustees 52–3
Children Act 1989 35–6
co-executorship 50, 91
co-ownership
  and inheritance 22–3, 28
  in Scotland 73
  and survivorship provisions
    20–1
codicils 49, 66–7
cohabitees 11, 12, 40, 58–60
  in Scotland 206, 208
confirmation (Scotland)
  192–205
  forms for 194–6, 197–8
  lodging 198–9
cousins 186, 189
creditors
  advertising for 118–19, 149
    in Northern Ireland 213
    in Scotland 203

payment of 153–5
    in Scotland 202
Crown, estate passing to 190, 208

death certificates 79, 90, 140, 166, 167
death grant 112
debts 116–19
    advertising for creditors 118–19, 149
    ordinary debts 202
    payment of
        in England 117–18
        in Scotland 202–3, 210
    priorities for creditors 117–18
    privileged debts 202
    secured debts 202
deeds of family arrangement 21, 24
deeds of variation 21, 24, 30
dependants, obligations to 40
    in Northern Ireland 215–16
    in Scotland 72
deponing in Scotland 198
deposit and registration of wills 65
destroying a will 68
disabled people and IHT 16
discretionary trusts 16
    and tax saving 23
disinheriting 39–40
    in Scotland 72
disposition (Scotland) 203
district valuer 100, 150
dividends 107, 169, 171
divorce 56, 69–70
    in Scotland 75, 206
docket (Scotland) 203–5
domicile, place of 9–10

employer, amounts owed by 133

engrossment 47
estate
    accounts 174–7
    administration of 80–179
    calculation of 36–7, 64, 94–109, 123–6
    distribution of 171–9
    insolvent 82, 117–18
        in Scotland 192
    life interest in 12, 38–9
    moveable 71, 72, 196, 210
    residue of 38, 174, 179
        in Scotland 196, 200–1, 210
    variation of 21–2
estate duty 15
ex-dividend shares 109, 134
execution (signing the will) 60–3
    in Scotland 74–5
executors 13, 31–5, 73
    administration of estate 80–179
    appointing 33–5, 50
    authority and duties of 33, 77–8, 84–5, 91
    co-executorship 50, 91
    husbands/wives as 33, 50
    keeping informed 64–5
    main beneficiary as 50
    not to witness will 60–1
    personal expenses 172
    renouncement 50, 92
        in Northern Ireland 213
        in Scotland 193
    in Scotland 73, 192, 193, 195, 199–200, 201
    as taxable entities 168
executors-dative (Scotland) 192, 206
executors-nominate (Scotland) 192, 193, 206
executorship account 122, 148, 171, 174

farms and agricultural land 14,
    18, 23
Finance Act 1986 16
foreign assets 129, 136
    in Scotland 196
funeral arrangements 12, 43, 48,
    89, 112, 136
    in Scotland 202, 210
furnishings (Scotland) 209

gifts 137–8
    birthday gifts 24
    'free from all taxes' 50–1
    and inheritance tax 16, 24–8
    small bequests 12, 18, 37,
        50–1
    to children 18
    to spouse 18
    wedding gifts 24–5
    see also lifetime gifts
gilt-edged securities 53–4, 159
Girobank accounts 96, 121
grandchildren 183, 187, 207
grandparents 11
grossing up calculations 29–30
guardians 12, 35–6, 50, 53, 66

hire purchase agreements 116,
    155
holograph will 75, 198
home-made wills 13, 82
household effects, valuation of
    113–16
    in Scotland 209
houses
    and Form IHT 37: 135
    and Form IHT 44: 136
    and Form PA5 128–9
    inheritance tax, instalments
        on 143
    joint ownership of 22–3,
        100–3
    making gifts of 22–3

outstanding mortgages on 90,
    102–3
registered 162–5
    in Northern Ireland 214–15
    in Scotland 204–5
renting out 39
sales and CGT 161
    in Scotland 193–4, 203–5, 209
tenancy-in-common 21,
    22–3, 28, 100–2, 184
transfer of 161–8
    in Northern Ireland 214
    in Scotland 203–5
unregistered 165–7
    in Northern Ireland 215
    in Scotland 204
valuation of 99–104
husbands/wives
    as executors 33, 50
    disinheriting 39–40
        in Scotland 72
    sample wills of 45–55, 56–8
    simultaneous deaths 41–2
        in Northern Ireland 212
    spouse predeceasing 41–2

illegitimacy and inheritance 37,
    181
income tax 112–13
    calculation of 169–70
    credits 177, 178
    on estate 168–70
    on legacy interest 173
    and lifetime gifts 16
    permitted deduction 168
    refunds 151
    return form (R59) 169
income tax deduction certificates
    177
Inheritance (Provision for
    Family and Dependants)
    Act 1975 82, 178, 190

claims under 178–9, 190, 207
Inheritance (Provision for
     Family and Dependants)
     (Northern Ireland) Order
     1977 220
inheritance tax (IHT) 7–8,
     15–30, 155–6
  and adult children 56–8
  calculation and tax savings
     19–24
  exemptions and reliefs 18
  finance for 119–23
  and household effects 115
  and intestate estates 181
  and joint ownership 101, 102
  nil-rate band 17, 21
  payment of 143–4, 156
  and pension schemes 111
  and probate 127
  and property valuation 100,
     101, 172
  rates 17
  rectification 150–2
  in Scotland 198
  seven-year rule 16–17
  and share sales 156–7
  small bequests and 50–1
  and stocks and shares 104
  survivorship provisions
     20–1
Inland Revenue 100, 108, 152,
     171
  accounting to 80, 151
  see also income tax;
     inheritance tax (IHT)
instructions for next-of-kin and
     executors 65
insurance companies 143
  see also life insurance
interest
  on bank accounts 122, 123,
     168, 169, 170

  on building society accounts
     126
  on delayed legacy payments
     173
  on inheritance tax 143
  in Scotland 205
intestacy 9–11
  and beneficiary predeceasing
     40–2
  and cohabitees 11, 12
  distribution on 180–191
  and married couples 10–11,
     182–6
  in Northern Ireland 215–20
  partial 41
  in Scotland 71, 200, 201–2,
     206–11
  and single people 11, 187–91
  and surviving children 10, 12,
     183
invalidation of wills 43
investments 12, 53–4, 173
  restrictions on 12, 52

jewellery, valuation of 114–15
  in Scotland 209
joint bank accounts 97–8
  in Scotland 194
joint property ownership 100–3
  and assent 166
  and form IHT 44: 139
  and inheritance tax 28
  of personal effects 113–14
  and probate 80
  in Scotland 193–4
joint tenancy 138
  and inheritance 22–3
  and intestacy 185
  in Scotland 73
  and survivorship provisions 21

land certificate 162, 165

Land Register for Scotland 204
Land Registry 80, 162–3
 fees 164
Land Registry assent Form 32
  (Northern Ireland) 214–15
Land Registry Form 100
  (Northern Ireland)
  214–15, 226–7
lapsed legacies 72
leasehold property 163–4, 167
legal advice, free (green form
  scheme) 14
legal rights (Scotland) 72, 76,
  203–4, 210
legal terminology 44
letter of request (Form
  CON41A) 157
letters of administration 32, 77,
  78, 119, 142–3, 145, 146,
  180, 181
life insurance 99
 decreasing term insurance
  16–17, 26–7
 policies and Form IHT 44:
  132–3, 136, 137
life interest 15, 38–9, 45, 82
 intestacy and 12
 property as 162
lifetime gifts
 example of 26–8
 exemptions 24–5
 and Form IHT 44: 137, 138
 and inheritance tax 16,
  24–30
 PETs 25–6
 and seven-year rule 16, 25
 tax on 25–6
Lloyd's underwriting syndicate
  14, 18, 23
London Gazette 118, 119, 149
London Stock Exchange 104–5,
  108–9, 158

mail redirection 90
marriage 58–9, 68–9
 revocation by 68–9
 in Scotland 75
marriage settlements 138
married couples
 and inheritance tax 18
 and intestacy 10–11
 married minors 212
matrimonial home questionnaire
  (PA5) 128–9
mental incapacity 31
mortgage debts 37, 90, 103, 135,
  136
 assent and 166
 certificates concerning 163,
  164, 165
 dischargement of 154
 in Scotland 205
 and house valuation 102–3
  in Scotland 205
 selling house to pay 161–2
moveable estate in Scotland 71,
  72, 196, 210
museums, gifts to 18

nation, gifts to the 18
National Savings 78, 79, 95
 and finance for IHT 120–1
 and Form IHT 44: 130, 140
 limit on holdings 147–8
nomination 79–80
Northern Ireland, wills and
  probate in 212–27
notaries public 198
Notice of Title (Scotland) 204

organ donation 50
overdrafts 89

paintings 115
partnership businesses 18

PAYE *see* income tax
pension schemes 109–11, 138–9
    state basic pension 111
personal effects 78
    distribution of 172–3
    valuation of 113–16
personal representatives 77
    see also administrators;
        executors
PETs *see* potentially exempt
        transfers
political parties, gifts to 18
potentially exempt transfers
        (PETs) 25–6
premium bonds 78, 95–6, 131,
        147
prior rights (Scotland) 207, 209,
        210
probate 77–86
    fees 140–1
    in Northern Ireland 214
    forms 119, 126–40
    in Northern Ireland 213–14
    grant of 77, 78, 144–6
    when not needed 78–80
probate application form (PA1)
        127–8
    in Northern Ireland 214
probate oath 141–2, 198
Probate Registry 7, 86, 119, 120,
        126–7, 140
property
    and Form IHT 37: 127, 135
    joint ownership 28, 80,
            100–3, 139
        in Scotland 73
    leasehold property 163–4, 167
    lifetime gift of 17–18, 28–9
    related property provisions 102
    rented accommodation 182
    see also houses
Public Trustee 35

    in Scotland 73

Real, Leasehold and Immoveable
        Property Schedule (IHT
        37) 127, 135
receipts for legacies 172–3
Register of Registrars 107
registered property 162–5
    in Northern Ireland 214–15
    in Scotland 204–5
Registry of Deeds (Northern
        Ireland) 215
relations 37, 82
    of the half blood 188
    tracing 82
rented accommodation 182
residuary beneficiary
    and inheritance tax 30
    spouse as 29
residue 38
    and beneficiaries predeceasing
            40–2
    and debt settlement 118
    distribution of 174, 179
reversions 134
revocation clauses 45–6
    and codicils 66–7

Scotland, wills and probate in
        71–6, 192–211
shares *see* stocks and shares
sheriff court 198, 201
single people and intestacy 11
    sample will of 55–6
sisters/brothers and intestacy 11,
        186
    in Northern Ireland 216
    in Scotland 207
solicitors 150
    as executors 34
    fees 82–3
        in Northern Ireland 213

green form scheme 14
lodging wills with 87
when to consult 14–15, 21,
    77, 81–2
  in Scotland 200
Somerset House 65
sound mind, being of 31
stamp duty 53, 159–60
state benefits 111–12
stepchildren 75
  in Scotland 207
Stock Exchange Daily Official List
    105
stock transfer forms (Con 40)
    158
stocks and shares 104–9
  bonus issue 124
  dividing up 157–8
  ex-dividend shares 109, 134
  family company shares 18, 23
  and Form IHT 40: 131–2
  gifts of 18
  gilts 161
  mislaid certificates 124–5,
    149–50
  recently privatised company
    shares 125–6
  selling 152–3
  transferring 156–60
  Treasury and Exchequer stock
    161
  valuation 105–9
    in Northern Ireland 213
surviving spouses
  as executors 33, 50
    in Scotland 199, 206
  and IHT 19
  and intestacy 180–6
  and matrimonial home 128–9
  and share in property 135
survivorship destination
    (Scotland) 73, 193, 203

survivorship provisions 20–1

tax deduction certificates 169,
    171
tenancies 135
tenancy-in-common 21, 22–3,
    28, 100–2, 184
testing clause (Scotland) 74
transfer of value 137
Trustee Act 1925 7, 52–3
trustee securities 53
trustees 32–3
  executors as 51
  guardians as 36, 53
  pension schemes 111
  in Scotland 73
  and use of income and capital
    52–3
trusts 138
  discretionary trusts 16, 23
  family trusts 81
  and intestacy 12
  and power of appointment 14
  and reversions 134
  'secret' trust 43
  'trust for sale' 51–2

uncles/aunts and intestacy 11,
    189
  in Northern Ireland 216
  in Scotland 208
unit trusts 108, 131, 158, 159
unmarried couples 12, 58–60,
    98, 114
  in Scotland 207
unregistered property 165–7
  in Northern Ireland 215
  in Scotland 204

variation of estate 21–2

wedding gifts 24–5

widowers and inheritance
    in Northern Ireland 216
    in Scotland 209–11
widows
    life interest of 12
    in Northern Ireland 216
    sample will of 88–9
    in Scotland 209–11
wills
    alterations in 65–6
    attestation clause 62
    codicils 49, 66–7
    depositing 65
    examples of 46–9, 54–60
    formal reading of 89
    holograph will 75, 198
    home-made 13, 82
    necessity for 11–12
    preparations before making
        36–8, 46–7
    and probate 140, 141–2
    revocation clauses in 45–6,
        49–50, 67
    revocation of 67–70
        in Scotland 75–6
    safekeeping of 63–5
    in Scotland 71–6
    setting out of 47–8
    signing 60–3
        in Scotland 74–5
    solicitors' fees for 14
    void 190
    witnesses 31, 60–1, 62–3
        in Scotland 74
    wording of 44–5
woodland property 18, 23